Baseball Crazy

Martyn Godfrey

James Lorimer & Company, Publishers,
Toronto, 1996

James Lorimer & Company Ltd. acknowledges with thanks the support of the Canada Council, the Ontario Arts Council and the Ontario Publishing Centre in the development of writing and publishing in Canada.

Cover illustration: Daniel Shelton

Canada Cataloguing in Publication Data

Godfrey, Martyn
    Baseball Crazy

(Sports stories)
ISBN 1-55028-513-0 (bound)
ISBN 1-55028-512-2 (pbk.)

I. Title.   II. Series: Sports stories (Toronto, Ont.).

PS8563.08165B32 1996   jC813'.54   C95-933263-4
PZ7.G63Ba 1996

James Lorimer & Company Ltd., Publishers
35 Britain Street
Toronto, Ontario
M5A 1R7

Printed and bound in Canada

Contents

A Great Idea

"Tell them you wear it to bed, Rob," Cheryl said. "Say you never take it off. Tell them you even shower in it."

"Give me a break. Who is going to believe I wear a baseball hat in the shower? I've got to say something that makes sense."

Cheryl leaned back on the kitchen chair and pushed her blond bangs out of her eyes. "I don't think so, guy. You've got to sound baseball crazy. Like a baseball nut. You have to sound like the ultimate Blue Jays fan."

I stared at the blank piece of paper, drummed my fingers on the table for a few seconds, then reread the ad on page three of that morning's *Toronto Star*.

Be a Special Batboy for the Toronto Blue Jays!

The Toronto Blue Jays Baseball Club wants to find a Special Batboy for spring training in Dunedin, Florida. If you're a boy between the ages of 11 and 14, you're invited to apply for the job.

Simply tell us, in 200 words or less, why you think you're the perfect batboy. If we like what you write, we'll invite you to Florida for spring break to help the Blue Jays players prepare for another World Series championship. We'll pay all your expenses. The only job qualification is a desire to be part of the first-class Blue Jays organization.

If you're interested, start writing. Entries must reach us by January 31. That's only two weeks from today, so don't delay!

"It's no use. I can't think of anything to write," I said.

"Hey, I've got an idea, Rob," Cheryl suggested. "Tell them you have got Gorfetter's Disease."

"Gorfetter's Disease? What's that?"

She shrugged. "I just made it up. Tell them it's a rare tropical disease you caught in Papua New Guinea."

"I've never been to Papua New Wherever."

"They won't know that. Tell them you only have a year to live and Gorfetter's disease makes your arms and legs drop off and you end up looking like a fish. Also, say your eyeballs roll out and—"

"Whoa!" I stopped her. "My eyeballs roll out? What are you talking about? Why would I want to write anything like that?"

"For sympathy. When the judges read how you're turning into fish-boy, they'll feel sorry for you and they'll pick you."

"Cheryl, that's stupid."

"You've got to make yourself stand out. If you say, *Dear Blue Jays, My name is Robert Carter. Pick me. I'm a nice guy. I'll do a good job,* they'll just chuck it in the *g* file."

"I can't lie."

"You're too honest, Rob."

"Too honest? How can somebody be too honest?"

Cheryl got up and helped herself to a soft drink from the fridge, then hopped up and sat on the counter. "Well, how about last September when Mr. Weis was handing out the math texts? You ended up with the teacher's copy, the one with all the answers in the back. What did you do? You told Mr. Weis. That was too honest."

"Weis would have found out."

"Maybe. Maybe not."

My father entered the kitchen. "Yo, Cheryl, how many times have I told you not to sit on the kitchen counter?"

"A hundred?" She smiled and my dad smiled back. When Cheryl smiles her eyes seem to have lights behind them. It's infectious. When she grins, you do the same.

Dad grabbed his own soda. "You finished the letter for the contest, Rob?"

"I haven't even started. I need major inspiration."

"Hey, I've been around long enough to know that creativity takes a lot of patience." My father is a studio musician. He plays backup for lots of big names in Toronto and New York. "Give it time." Dad headed back into the living room.

"There's something I've always wondered about, Rob," Cheryl said. "How come your father is so cool and you're such a nerd?"

"I'm a nerd?"

"I'm kidding." She looked at her watch. "I think I'll go to the mall. I'll come back later, okay?"

"Maybe I'll be finished the letter by then."

"I'm looking forward to seeing how you answer that sexist ad."

"Sexist?"

She grabbed her jacket from the back of the chair. "They're asking for a batboy, not a batgirl. It isn't fair. Girls should get the same chance. Girls can pick up baseball bats just as good as boys."

"Sure they can. But I don't think the players would appreciate a batgirl helping out in the locker room. That's where the showers and bathrooms are."

Cheryl stared into space for a moment. "Now that would be interesting. Bye. I'm gone."

I heard Cheryl say goodbye to Dad, the front door open and close, and suddenly the kitchen seemed very empty. And the blank page was just as empty. I was overcome with a feeling of *I don't have a snowball's chance in a pizza oven of winning*. There'd be thousands and thousands of guys entering the contest.

Then again, somebody had to win. And what a prize. A week at spring training with the Toronto Blue Jays. It was better than winning the lottery.

I've played minor hockey on rep teams. I'm a pretty good goalie in soccer. But I'm nothing special, just one of the *okay* guys. But baseball is something else. I've been on elite teams since fourth grade. It's a sport I have a feel for. I'm not bragging. Everybody has a special skill in something. Some of us do good in school. Others know how to play the piano or dance or sing or whatever. I once read a book about a girl who was a natural at jumping her BMX over garbage cans. Every person in our class can do one thing better than someone else.

My talent is baseball. I love to hit a curve or a fastball. And I can throw them too, no sweat. I know how tough it is to make it as a pro ball player. But ever since I saw my first Blue Jays game, I knew pro ball was where I wanted to be. Being a Special Batboy seemed like a good step on that road. I'd get to meet the players and coaches.

I reread the contest ad for the twenty-fifth time. Like Cheryl said, I had to write something to make my two hundred words stand out. But how could I do that? Creative writing was definitely not one of my special skills.

And then it hit me!

The brain wave.

***

It took me an hour and a half to finish. I had to rewrite the thing seven times to get it exactly the way I wanted it, exactly perfect. As soon as I completed the last line, I folded the paper, shoved it into my pocket, grabbed my jacket and headed to the local mall.

Calling the local plaza a mall is too generous. There are a few stores, but the big attraction is the bowling alley/pool room/video arcade called Big Chuck's. One of Cheryl's favorite activities is dropping coins into the games. She's so good I've seen her last an afternoon on five bucks.

Big Chuck's was crowded with a bowling tournament and the regular punkers and bangers playing billiards. The arcade was just as crowded. I noticed a mob of kids around a Mortal Kombat 4 machine. In the middle of the group was a blond head.

I eased into the crowd. Cheryl glanced at me for a fraction of a second. "Hi, Rob. I'm on a tear."

"I haven't seen anybody get this far so fast," one of the kids praised.

"Can I talk to you?" I asked. "Somewhere quiet."

She nodded. "Who wants to take over?"

A skinny kid moved in front of the machine and joystick. Cheryl took my arm and directed me out the door.

"I didn't mean right away," I said. "You could have finished the game."

"It's cool. Let's go to McDonald's and get a shake."

We jogged across the street, entered the restaurant and bought a couple of chocolate shakes. Cheryl steered me toward the little kids' section. She chose a table under the plastic statue of Ronald McDonald. I squeezed my legs under the tiny table. "Why are we sitting here?"

"Float with it, Rob. We're in junior high. We're allowed to act strange. Hormones. Puberty. Enjoy it. Now what's up?"

"The Blue Jays thing. I've finished. I want you to read it."

"Did you use Gorfetter's Disease?"

"Of course not."

"Good, because I have a better idea. Tell them your folks were killed in a plane crash and you had to quit school in the sixth grade to support the quintuplets."

"Right. As if anyone would believe that. I got a terrific idea and I didn't need to lie. You see, I figured the Jays would get a truckload of letters all saying the same thing: how much the guy wants to be Special Batboy. So I realized I had to do something no one else would do. I wrote a poem."

She placed her shake on the table and stared into my face. "You what?"

"I wrote a poem on why I want to be part of the Blue Jays." I reached into my jacket pocket and unfolded the paper.

"You wrote a poem?"

"Don't sound so surprised. It's a good poem."

"You wrote a *good* poem?"

"Stop that." I gave her the paper. "Read it and tell me how great I am."

She slowly scanned the page.

"So what do you think?" I asked impatiently.

Cheryl held up her hand. "Just a sec." When she got to the end, she glanced at me, then back at the paper. "Rob, how can I say this?" She looked at me sympathetically. "Okay, listen. I'll read it out loud. Pretend you're hearing it for the first time. Pretend you didn't write it. Tell me what you honestly think about this poem."

"Are you telling me you don't like it?"

She opened her mouth to say something, then quickly shook her head. She took a sip of her shake and cleared her throat. "Just listen," she repeated. "Here goes…

I Want to Be Part of the Blue Jays

Hey, hey, hey,
I want to be part of the Blue Jays.

No matter what you say,
I want to be part of the Blue Jays.

Go ahead and make my day,
Make me one of the Toronto Blue Jays.

I love to run and I love to play
That I am one of the Toronto Blue Jays.

Chickens cluck and horses neigh
Whenever they see one of the Blue Jays.

Red, orange, purple, grey,
Blue is our favorite color say the Jays.

I'll be fast, no feet of clay,
When I pick up bats for all the Jays.

Come what may,
I want to help pick up bats for the Jays.

I promise I won't sleep in the hay;
I'll hustle for the Blue Jays.

Hey, hey, hey,
I want to be part of the Blue Jays.

"Well?" Cheryl asked. "How did it hit you?"

"It's terrific."

She sighed. "Rob, it stinks. This is, without doubt, the worst poem I've ever read."

"What's wrong with it?"

"Hey, hey, hey. And it gets worse after that."

"It flows together and makes sense."

"'Chickens cluck and horses neigh' makes sense?"

"Writing a poem is a good idea."

"It's a great idea," she agreed and twirled the straw in her milkshake. "Now let's figure out how we're going to fix up this poem."

"I don't want to fix up the poem!" I snapped. "I like the poem. I'm going to send it in the way it is."

Cheryl held up her hands. "Peace, man. Okay, it's a great poem. I'm sure your poem will win. I was wrong." She drained the milkshake. "You want me to input this on my Mac and run off a printed copy?"

"You read my mind."

She folded the paper and shoved it into her jacket. "I'll drop by after supper."

I should have known better. Cheryl and I had been friends for so long, I should have known better.

2

Spiders

My dad and I were watching the Leafs game on TV when Cheryl opened the front door, kicked off her boots, sauntered into the living room and flopped on the couch between us.

"Hi, guys. What's the score?"

"4–1 for Detroit," I told her.

"Is that good or bad?" she wondered. Then she said to Dad, "Say, Mr. Carter, do you know when Alanis Morissette is going to record her new album yet?"

"Next month maybe," Dad answered.

"You'll remember to invite me into the studio one day when she does?" she pleaded.

Dad smiled. "I promise."

They gave each other high fives.

The second period of the hockey game ended. "You want to make some popcorn?" I asked Cheryl. She nodded and we went into the kitchen.

I threw a packet of low-calorie popcorn into the microwave.

Cheryl scrunched her nose. "How come you don't buy real popcorn? That Lite stuff has no taste. You should get the double-butter, extra-salt kind."

"You know, I worry about your diet. You eat too much junk food."

"I worry about your diet," she teased. "You're such a dip."

"Thanks. With friends like you, who needs enemies?"

"A cliché response. So like you. I printed out your poem."

"Great. I'll mail it tomorrow."

"No need," she said. "I dropped it in the mailbox at the mall. There's a pick-up at eight tomorrow morning. I figured you'd want it to get there a.s.a.p."

"Did you include my name and address?"

"Of course. Hey, I have some good news and some great news. Remember I told you about my Grandpa Robinson who used to live in Edmonton? I told you he moved to Florida two years ago after my grandma died. Well, the good news is my grandfather called after supper. He's going to pay to fly me down to Florida to visit him for spring break."

"Super."

"He lives in North Redington Beach. That's just south of Clearwater. He says Clearwater is next to Dunedin where the Jays spring train, a twenty-minute drive. So, if you win the contest, I can come watch you."

"More than super."

She winked. "And, this is the great-news part, Grandpa told me he'd pay for a plane ticket for a friend. I told him I'd like to bring my boyfriend and he said fine. That's you, big guy. So even if you don't win the contest, you can still go to Florida and see a couple of Jays spring training games."

"Your grandfather is going to pay for me? You're kidding."

She grinned. "My father says Grandpa's place is huge. He has four extra bedrooms. You'll love it. Dad says you can lie in bed and listen to the waves on the beach. Do you think your folks will let you come?"

"Of course. Thanks, Cheryl. That's…wow, spring break in Florida. Thanks." Then I added, "I only hope I'm working for the Jays at the same time."

"Well, your poem stands a good chance. You want to hear something funny?"

The popcorn began to pop.

"I stopped at Big Chuck's for a quick game on my way over," Cheryl went on. "You know Henry Wong?"

"Sure, he was in my seventh-grade class last year."

"He played this great trick on Weird Willy."

"Weird Willy? Do you know I once offered Willy some pistachio nuts and he chewed them up, shell and all. When he swallowed, he said, 'These things are really crunchy.' I'd never play a trick on Willy."

"It was so funny," she went on. "You know those spiders you see in Big Chuck's? The black ones that scoot across the floor? Henry found four of them. Then when he saw Willy buying a burger from the snack bar, he asked me to go talk to Willy for a minute to distract him."

"Why you?"

"'Cause everyone knows Weird Willy has the hots for me."

"He does?"

She stared at me for a few seconds. "Sometimes you're so thick. Anyway, while I was talking with Willy, Henry went to the counter, got the burger and put those spiders under the bun."

"That's, er, that's..."

"Great, huh? I told Willy I had to go and he went back to the snack bar, grabbed the hamburger and took a huge bite. Then he got this funny look. I was laughing so hard I thought I'd pee myself. Willy decided to check why his food tasted so strange. He lifted the bun and saw what was left of the spiders."

My stomach heaved.

"What was *left* of the spiders," Cheryl repeated. "Willy went this funny off-yellow color. Thinking about it makes me..." She couldn't finish. She buried her head in her hands and laughed herself out. It took over a minute for her chuckles to wind down.

I took the swollen popcorn bag out of the microwave. "Popcorn's ready."

She glanced at me through her fingers. "You're not laughing."

"That was an awful thing to do to Willy. How could you be a part of it? Think of the germs on those spiders."

"Sometimes I wonder why you and I are friends," she said. "We're so different." She thought for a moment. "Maybe that's why I like you so much. When's the next school dance?"

"I don't know. After spring break, I think."

"When it comes, would you like to go with me?"

"To the dance? Me and you?"

"Yeah, Rob. Me and you."

"Would we have to dance?"

"Go to the dance to *dance*?" she pondered. "No, we'll go to the dance to ride buffaloes. What a stupid question. What do you think we're going to do?"

I ripped the popcorn packet over a large bowl. "I don't know how to dance."

"You just have to hold me and move your feet. You think you can do that?"

For some reason, I felt embarrassed. "I guess."

"Relax, Rob," Cheryl said. "Don't get hyper about it. I'd like to go to the dance with you. I hope you feel the same way. Let me know, okay?" She grabbed a handful of popcorn and stuffed it into her mouth. "See yu, Rub. I gut to gu babusut my liddle sitter."

"You have to babysit your little sister?" I said. "Okay. Thanks again for mailing my poem."

She seemed to shrink a little. "Nu prublum." She swallowed. "It was a good poem. I'll call you tomorrow."

3

Something about Florida

Three weeks later, Cheryl and I spent part of the afternoon playing games at Big Chuck's. We took a break at the snack bar.

"Okay," Cheryl said. "What's wrong, Rob? You're acting like you're only half here. What's on your mind?"

"As if you don't know," I replied. "It's the batboy thing. The contest closed last week. Every day I've been rushing home to check the mail and the answering machine. Absolutely zip. I guess I didn't win. They must have picked somebody by now."

"Maybe. Then again, maybe not. There has to be a ton of letters for them to read. I haven't heard of anybody else winning either."

"You're sure you mailed my poem?"

"That's the tenth time you've asked and it's starting to bug me. For the tenth time, I mailed the letter, Rob."

"You put my name on it?"

"For the tenth time, I put your name and address at the top of the page."

"You didn't drop the envelope as you were putting it into the box?"

"I mailed it!" she shouted.

A couple of elementary school kids at the next table checked us out, no doubt curious why Cheryl was yelling. "It must have got lost in the post office. I've heard that happens sometimes."

"Your poem got there, Rob," she assured me. "Give them time."

"I suppose so."

"Hey, even if you lose, you don't. You're going to spend spring break with my grandfather. You'll like him. Grandpa is seventy, but he looks twenty years younger and he laughs and jokes around like a kid. We'll go see the Jays. Even if you lose, you win."

"I suppose. I'm looking forward to spending time with you in Florida, Cheryl."

"That's what I want to hear. I like it when you say nice things to me."

"Nice things?"

"Speaking of which, Rob, do you know what day it is today?"

I looked at my watch. "February 14th. Exactly one week after the close of the Special Batboy contest."

"Yeah, but what else is February 14th? What special day is it?"

"A few weeks before the batboy winner goes to Florida to help out the greatest baseball team of all time."

"Come on, Dumbo!" Cheryl said. "It's Valentine's Day."

"Big deal."

"Big deal? That's all you have to say? This is one of the greatest days of the year. It's dedicated to the most powerful emotion human beings have. Love."

"What has that got to do with the Blue Jays?"

"Nothing, Bozo. Do you know what Kevin O'Keeffe gave Linda Donnish today? No, of course you wouldn't. He gave her a dozen roses. Had them delivered right in the middle of gym class. Do you know how much roses cost?"

"No."

"Figures. They cost a fortune. Linda got all embarrassed and started crying. Things like that really move me."

"It was a nice thing to do," I said.

"Sure was. How come you didn't get me anything for Valentine's Day, Rob? I mean, even a card would have been appreciated."

"Because Valentine's Day is for people who like each other."

"And you don't like me?"

"Course I do. But it's not like you're my girlfriend or anything."

"Am I a girl?"

"Yes."

"Am I your friend?"

"Yes."

"Maybe you should think about it a little more," she suggested.

"What do you mean?"

"Nothing. I have to get going; it's my turn to make supper tonight."

I walked Cheryl home, went back to my place and flopped on my bed to read the latest Paul Kropp novel. After a few minutes, Mom poked her head into the room. "Hi, honey," she said.

"Hi, Mom. How's it going?"

"Busy," she answered. "Never become an accountant. Tax time is murder. You'll never guess what I did today. I borrowed Dad's car and stopped to get gas. When I went to pull the little lever beside the seat to open the gas cap, I pulled the wrong one and opened the trunk. The trunk swung open and nearly hit the gas jockey on the chin. Why do they put those switches so close together?"

"Beats me."

"Are you feeling okay, Rob? You've been so mopy the last few days."

"It's just the batboy thing. It's been a week since the contest closed. The Blue Jays must have picked somebody else."

She smiled. "Oh, I forgot. Speaking of the Blue Jays, there was a phone call for you this afternoon from a Mr. Jim Dennis. He said he was the Public Relations Manager for the Toronto Blue Jays."

I forgot how to breathe.

"He said he wanted to speak to you. Of course, I told him you weren't home."

"What did he want?" I said the sentence as one word.

"I don't know. I didn't ask."

"You didn't ask? Somebody from the Blue Jays called and you didn't ask what he wanted?"

She shook her head. "He did say something about Florida." Mom handed me a piece of paper. "Here's his number. He wants you to call him."

"Something about Florida?" I jumped off the bed, grabbed the paper, hugged my mother and dashed downstairs to the phone.

"Take a couple of deep breaths before you speak to him," Mom called.

I sat on the couch, placed the phone on my lap, fumbled with the paper, then punched in the wrong number. I redialed and followed Mom's instructions. Deep breath. Deep breath.

"Hello, Jim Dennis, Toronto Blue Jays Baseball Club."

"Mr. Dennis? My name is Robert Carter and my mom said—"

"Ah, Rob," Mr. Dennis interrupted. "I think I have some good news for you. How would you like to spend spring break in Florida with the Jays?"

"Yay!" I shouted into his ear. "Yaaaayyyy!"

***

A half-hour later I pounded on Cheryl's front door. Her father answered. "Howdy, Rob. Cheryl's downstairs."

The drum-thump of rock music thundered from the family room. I kicked off my boots and headed downstairs. Cheryl was lying on her stomach on the carpet in front of the CD player. "Hey, Cheryl." She didn't hear me, so I shouted, "Hey, Cheryl!"

She twisted around, sat up and turned down the volume. "What? I've never seen you smile like that before. You're glowing. Did you—"

I bobbed my head. "Yeah, I won. Can you believe it? I hoped I'd win, but I didn't really think...I won, Cheryl. My poem was picked. I won the contest. I'm going to be the Special Batboy. I'm going to Florida to help the Jays."

Cheryl hopped to her feet, bounced toward me, threw her hands around my neck and planted a kiss on my cheek. "Congrats, big guy! All right!"

"They said my poem was very creative."

"Creative! They did?"

"I told you it was a good poem."

"A good poem? Creative? Think of that. Awesome. That's wonderful news, Rob. I'm so happy for you. Excellent!" She paused. "Wait a sec. How come you haven't blown up?"

"Blown up?"

"You should be dancing on the ceiling. How come you're not ripping your lungs out?"

"I already did that at my place," I explained.

"Still, knowing you, you should be singing. What's up?"

"There's a tiny bit of a hassle."

"A hassle?"

"I need an adult to accompany me in Florida," I said. "That's part of the deal. Mr. Dennis, the guy from the Jays, said I need a chaperone."

"Why can't your folks go?"

"Dad can't do it because he's in studio. Mom's too busy because it's tax time. So—"

"So you want me to pretend I'm your mom and go to Florida with you?" Cheryl said. "No problem, my son."

"Maybe your grandfather can help me. Do you think he'd agree to be my chaperone while I'm down there? He'll just have to, you know, hang around with me. I told the Blue Jays guy I was going to stay with him anyway."

"Of course he will," Cheryl exclaimed. "He'll love it." She kissed my cheek again. "Way to go. We're on the Blue Jays."

***

Three weeks after that, Cheryl, Mr. Jim Dennis and I caught Air Canada flight 910 from Pearson Airport in Toronto to Tampa International Airport in Florida. I was so excited I kept babbling about the Blue Jays players' statistics to Mr. Dennis. He pretended to be interested for a half-hour, then told me he had work to do and took out his laptop.

After the meal, Cheryl asked, "How long have we known each other, Rob?"

"Forever," I answered. "Since kindergarten. Why?"

"How long have we been friends?"

"Since fourth grade. Why?"

"Remember how you used to get teased back then, because your best friend was a girl?"

"It didn't bother me. Not all that much anyway. I could tell some of the guys on my ball team were kind of jealous."

"They were?"

"Yeah, they wanted a good-looking girl cheering for them too."

"How come you didn't tell me this before?"

"I didn't think of it."

She slapped my shoulder.

"Ow!"

"Sorry. Wait a sec. What did you just say? Did you just call me a good-looking girl? Do you think that?"

"Of course."

"How come you never told me that before?"

"You never asked."

She looked up at the ceiling of the cabin and sighed. "Why is he so thick?" she whispered to herself.

"Did I say something wrong?"

"Not really. It's just that I wish you'd say something right."

"I don't understand."

"Rob, now that we're in eighth grade, do you feel any different about me?"

"No, you're still my best friend."

"What I mean is, when you look at me, do I look different in any way?"

"I don't think so," I muttered.

"That's what I thought." She sounded sad as she turned to Jim Dennis and pointed to his computer. "You got any games on that thing, Mr. Dennis?"

***

As the plane touched down, I peered out the window. "There's one," I told Cheryl.

"There's one what?"

"A palm tree. There's a palm tree. See it?"

She squinted over my shoulder. "Right, a palm tree."

"I've never seen a palm tree in real life before."

"Right, a palm tree."

"Look, there's another one by the fence."

"Right, two palm trees. Geez, my life got exciting all of a sudden."

***

Cheryl's grandfather met us in the terminal. Cheryl and Grandpa spent a minute of major hugging. Cheryl was right about him; Mr. Robinson certainly didn't act all that old. Or look it. He was in great shape and had hardly any grey hair. After the introductions, Cheryl told Grandpa what a great ball player I was.

"I'm not that good, Mr. Robinson," I told him.

"Mr. Robinson?" her grandfather reacted. "I don't like that. My name is Dave. If you feel uncomfortable using my first name, call me Grandpa like Cheryl does."

"Okay, thanks, Grandpa." It felt weird calling someone I'd met only two minutes before, Grandpa.

Mr. Dennis explained how I had to be at the stadium every day except Thursday, when I had a day off. Grandpa assured Mr. Dennis he'd have me at work on time and that he was looking forward to the week too. Then Mr. Dennis reached into his flight bag and pulled out a nylon Blue Jays jacket. He handed it to me. On the sleeves were the twin decals Batboy. "Awesome," I said as I slipped it on.

"Suits you," Cheryl said.

"See you tomorrow at ten," Mr. Dennis said to me. "We have a game against the Red Sox in the evening. Rob, you'll be in the dugout. And the rest of us will have seats in a private box. I hope everyone can join us?"

"We'd be delighted," Grandpa replied. "That's most generous."

"Is there any doubt?" Cheryl said. "I want to watch the Robster do his thing."

**

Cheryl's grandfather owned a mini-mansion. At first I couldn't believe it. "I didn't think the house would be like this. I thought it would be some kind of condo."

"Grandpa was a stock broker," Cheryl whispered into my ear when she saw my stunned expression. "He made a few bucks."

"A few?" I whispered back.

Just like Cheryl had promised, my guest bedroom faced the ocean, and as I unpacked my suitcase, I heard the waves of the Gulf of Mexico lapping the white sand beach. Grandpa took us for a long walk along the shore before supper, and we spent a ton of time searching the beach for sea shells. By six o'clock, it was dark.

As Grandpa barbecued shrimp for supper, Cheryl told him what she'd been doing for the year. He told us how wonderful it was to be retired in North Redington Beach and how he missed Grandma every day. Then we played Scrabble until bedtime.

I lay in bed listening to the ocean, too excited to sleep. I thought about how I was going to meet all my heroes in the morning. How I was going to be able to speak to Edgar Sanchez. Pick up Josh Martin's bat. Take new baseballs to the bullpen for Cy Young winner, Tom Washington. Tomorrow, I'd actually wear an official Toronto Blue Jays uniform. Who would have dreamed? The whole week was going to be over-poweringly awesome.

Little did I know how overpoweringly awesome.

4

Welcome to the Blue Jays

The next morning, Grandpa pulled his car in front of Grant Field, the stadium where the Blue Jays play their spring training games, at a quarter to ten. Mr. Dennis stood by the main gate talking to a group of security guards. He waved to us, spent another few seconds instructing the guards about something and walked over to the car.

"You're a little early," Mr. Dennis said as I got out. "Good. It shows enthusiasm. We like that. How are you feeling, Rob?"

"Scared," I said. "More than scared. My fingers and toes are tingling."

"Enjoy it," Mr. Dennis instructed. "That's excitement. In your whole life, you're going to get this excited maybe two or three times. Savor the moment, as the saying goes."

"I'll try."

"I'll leave Rob with you," Grandpa said. "I'll bring Cheryl back for the game."

After Mr. Robinson drove away, Mr. Dennis escorted me past a security guard into an office, where I was introduced to Mrs. Doris Pitman. "Doris is our promotion person," Mr. Dennis explained. "She's in charge of getting fans into the spring training games."

"Not much of a job really," Mrs. Pitman said. "There's nearly five thousand seats and most of the time we're sold out. A lot of Canadians plan their vacations so they can watch the Blue Jays in Dunedin."

"What better vacation could there be?" I replied.

She smiled. "By the way, I thought your poem was wonderful. We've decided to include it in our new program so all the fans can enjoy it. It should be printed by Friday."

"Hey, hey, hey, I want to be part of the Blue Jays," I recited the poem's first verse.

Mrs. Pitman acted confused.

"Hey, hey, hey, I want to be part of the Blue Jays," I repeated.

"Er, yes, I…" Mrs. Pitman mumbled. "Whatever you say."

"Come on, Rob," Mr. Dennis said. "Let's go into the inner sanctum."

"The inner sanctum?" I wondered. "What's that?"

"A fancy word used by the people who have a pass to enter the restricted area," he said. "Where the players are."

***

We exited through the back door of the office into a grassy area surrounded by high, steel-paneled walls. The ground was occupied by wooden picnic tables.

"This is where we eat lunch," Mr. Dennis said.

A guy, about twenty years old or so, dressed in a white uniform, unlocked a door in the wall and entered, carrying a large food cooler. "Hey, Mr. Dennis," he called. "How's it flying?"

"Not bad, Gerald. What's for lunch today?"

"Subs, man," Gerald answered. "All kinds of different subs. Makes me hungry just thinking about them." He put the cooler on the grass, unlocked the door to the locker room, picked up the food again and entered the building.

"Gerald works for our local caterer," Mr. Dennis told me. "Besides the food, he keeps the fridges stocked with juice and sodas."

"Sounds like a great job."

"I suppose." Mr. Dennis reached into his pocket and handed a key to me. "Here, this opens the clubhouse door. You might have to open up or close down one day. Don't lend it to anyone. It also opens the special cupboard."

"The special cupboard? What's that?"

"I'll let Sam show you. Let's go meet the players."

"Meet the players. I'm in heaven."

We followed Gerald the caterer into the Blue Jays clubhouse. The place was buzzing with conversation and laughter. The Blue Jays players were dressed in their spring practice uniforms. Some were doing stretching exercises, others were taping wrists and knees. The whole place felt full of electricity, like something important was happening.

"Holy," I muttered.

Mr. Dennis clapped his hands a couple of times to get everybody's attention. The noise level dropped to near silence as everyone turned to face us. I felt not only scared, but somewhat intimidated. Baseball superstars stared at me. I dropped my head and studied the laces on my runners.

"Gentlemen," Mr. Dennis announced. "I'd like to introduce you to Robert Carter, who likes to be called Rob. Rob is from Toronto. He won the Special Batboy contest and is here for spring break."

I lifted my head and smiled as much as I could. "Hi," I said meekly.

Suddenly, the room exploded into noise again. Fifty players, trainers and coaches called out their welcome. And then Mr. Dennis led me along the lockers to meet everyone. I shook hands with the men I'd admired from the seats of the Sky Dome and from my couch in front of the TV. Mike

Masdle, Josh Martin, Steve Walton, Tom Washington, Frank O'Keeffe, Edgar Sanchez, Xavier Fernandez — all the superstars who had won two World Series, the guys whose baseball cards I kept in plastic pockets in my collector albums.

It would be an understatement to say I was stunned.

The last person I met was Clarence Rivers, the Jays number two catcher. "You got a great smile, kid," he told me.

"Now we go to work, Rob," Mr. Dennis declared. He directed me into the equipment room, patted my back, said goodbye and left.

A middle-aged man with one of the largest pot bellies I've ever seen approached me. "Hi, I'm Sam Morris, the equipment manager. You must be our winner."

"Rob Carter, sir."

He grinned and nodded in the direction of a tall, red-haired boy about my age, dressed in a Blue Jays uniform. He was sorting through a bucket of scuffed baseballs. "This is Clyde Pitman, my second in command. You probably met his mom in the office. Clyde is our usual batboy down here in Florida. You'll be taking his job for the week."

Clyde and I nodded a greeting at each other. He didn't seem all that happy to see me. Of course, I could understand that. If I was the full-time batboy, I wouldn't want somebody taking my job, even for a week.

Mr. Morris slapped my shoulder. "You ready to get to work, Rob?"

"You bet. I've dreamed about this for weeks."

"Good. Let's try to find you the batboy uniform." He began to search through a rack of uniforms against the far wall. After he checked it once, he checked it again. "Strange." He scratched his paunch. "I can't find the other batboy uniform." He called to the regular batboy, "You seen it, Clyde?"

"Sure," Clyde answered. "I sent it out yesterday. It's being cleaned."

Mr. Morris thumped his forehead and scratched his gut more vigorously. "Now I remember. Stupid me." He returned his attention to the uniforms. "We'll have to find you something for today." He pulled a hanger and suit from the rack and offered them to me. "This is an extra for Vito Lariano. He's the smallest player on the team, so I guess it will be a close fit. You can wear it for now, Rob. You got Locker 45. You can change there."

When I walked back into the dressing room, it was empty; the players and coaches had left for their morning workout. Locker 45 turned out to be a bench and some panels with clothes hooks and three shelves. There was nothing to lock. I changed clothes. Instantly, I knew Sam had made a mistake. The uniform belonged to a player a lot larger than Vito Lariano. You could fit three and a half of me inside it. My feet only reached the knees, fifteen inches of sleeve dangled past my wrist and the belt went around my waist twice. I couldn't find any punched holes to tighten the buckle, so I had to scrunch the waist in my hand to keep the pants from falling down.

"Looks good," Clyde the batboy said from behind me.

"You're joking, right?" I pushed up the sleeves so my hands were free. "I didn't know the Blue Jays had anybody who was ten feet tall and weighed a thousand pounds."

"It's a little loose, but it fits okay."

Clyde obviously needed glasses.

"I read your poem," Clyde told me. "I usually hate poetry, but yours was okay."

I tried to roll up the pant legs without dropping the pants.

"How's it going?" Sam appeared behind Clyde and studied my uniform.

"I think there's been a mistake." I smiled. "This is way too big for me."

Sam frowned. "What are you talking about? Looks fine to me."

I stared at a pant leg trailing across the tile floor. "The shirt goes past my knees," I joked.

"Don't get lippy," Sam said.

Lippy? "I wasn't being rude, sir. It's just that the uniform is way too big for me. I must look stupid."

"Looks fine to me," Sam snarled.

"Me too," Clyde added. "Like I said, it's a little big, but not by much."

Maybe they both needed glasses.

"Where's that new batboy?" a voice shouted from the doorway to the dugout.

Josh Martin, the Jays left fielder and the most valuable player in the last World Series, blocked the doorway with his hands planted on his hips.

"He's right here, Josh," Sam said.

Josh strode toward me. "I got a job for you to do, kid. I left my favorite bat in center field. Go get it for me."

"I, er…" I waved a hand across my far-too-large uniform.

"Now!" Josh Martin thundered. "When I want my favorite bat, I want it right away. Go get it now."

"Yes, sir."

"I'd put on the speed, if I were you," Sam Morris warned.

I stared up at the big left fielder. He folded his arms across his chest and flared his nostrils. "What's taking you so long?"

I dashed out of the locker room.

I fumbled my way out of the dugout and onto the field. Here I was, living out a dream, standing on the same field as the Blue Jays, and I felt awful. Things were definitely not going the way I thought they would. I'm not sure what I had expected, but I never dreamed I'd be forced to wear a ridiculous uniform, be called lippy by one of the trainers and be barked at by one of my heroes. Strange, Josh Martin seemed so friendly when he was interviewed on TV.

I stopped to roll up the extra yard of pant legs.

"What are you doing?" Josh Martin yelled from the dugout doorway. "I said I want my bat now. I'm starting to get mad!"

I began to run across the infield. A groundskeeper was raking the pitcher's mound. She looked puzzled as I bounded past, clutching my waist and trying not to trip over my pants. I ran as quickly as I could, despite the handicap. By the time I'd covered the outfield and raced to the warning track, I was out of breath.

Josh Martin's favorite bat was leaning against the wall directly under the 400ft/121.9m sign. I grabbed it with my left hand, tightened the grip on my belt with my right, twisted around and headed back to the dugout. I saw Josh Martin waiting for me, wearing an angry scowl. Several other players had stopped their pepper game to watch me. I tried to run faster.

Halfway to the infield, my left pant leg unrolled and caught under my shoe. I tucked the bat under my left armpit and tried to adjust the pants on the fly. As I did, the other leg unrolled. Thrown off balance by the wads of uniform under my sneakers, I pitched forward. I threw out my left arm in an attempt to regain my balance. The bat dropped between my feet, tripped me, and I did a lip stand in shallow center.

To stop the grass from painting my face, I had to use both hands to break the fall. Of course, that meant I couldn't hold up my pants. And so I lay flat out, with the pants bunched around my ankles. Instantly, there was a wall of applause from the Blue Jays. Every player on the field had stopped their practice and clapped loudly as I struggled to my feet and yanked up the pants.

Josh Martin jogged out toward me. To my surprise, he was wearing a broad grin. He took his bat, then tousled my hair. "Welcome to the Blue Jays, Rob," he said with a hearty laugh.

I looked at him for a moment, then at the other cheering players. "What's going on?"

"That was your initiation," Josh Martin explained. "Everyone new to the club has to be initiated."

"You mean, this is some kind of joke? You're not mad at me?"

"Course not."

"This uniform is some kind of trick? Sam Morris isn't angry at me?"

He chuckled. "Sam and I have our faults, but meanness isn't one of them. We had that huge uniform made a couple of seasons ago to initiate the new batboys. Sam set you up. Then I came over and started chewing you out. It's part of the joke. Clyde didn't get past second base before he lost his pants." He patted my shoulder. "Now you're official. You're one of us."

"I am?"

"You passed the test, Rob," Josh Martin affirmed. "You're on the Blue Jays."

"All right." I smiled. "I'm one of the Jays."

***

The groundskeeper winked at me on my return trip to the locker room. "Nice legs," she said.

Even though my butt had been the butt of a practical joke, and even though I must have looked ridiculous, I felt pretty good, like I'd been accepted by the team.

Yancy Hutchins, the Jays manager, appeared. "Okay, gentlemen," he shouted. "Let's hit the outfield. I want twenty minutes."

"Find a spot," one of the coaches yelled.

The team hustled into the outfield, spread out and began running on the spot. "Push ups!" the coach hollered. Instantly the team fell to its collective hands and started pumping.

When I reached the dugout, Sam Morris was waiting for me. "You're a good sport, Rob. Let's go get you a real uniform. Then we'll show you the ropes."

5

Keys

After I changed into a regular uniform, I stood in front of the locker room mirror. "You look pretty good," I said to myself. "No, you look great. You're a natural. One day you'll be standing here as a player. One day people will collect your baseball card."

I watched Clyde's reflection walk up behind me. "You looked really funny, Poet."

"I heard you didn't get to second base before you lost your pants."

"Yeah, but I didn't look as stupid as you did, Poet."

"Why are you calling me Poet?"

"Cause you like to write poetry."

"I don't like to write poetry. I wrote a poem. One poem only. Please don't call me Poet."

Sam Morris's reflection appeared beside Clyde's. "Go finish sorting that bucket of balls, Clyde. It's almost batting practice." Clyde did as he was told. Then Sam said to me, "You look much better now, Rob. You look like you belong."

I turned around so I could see the numbers on the back of my uniform in the mirror, 00. "One day there will be real numbers there," I said. "One day I'm going to play for this team."

"And when you do, I'll ask you to help me initiate the new batboy. But right now, let's teach you about the batboy job. Did Jim give you a front-door key?"

I patted my pocket. "It's right here. Mr. Dennis told me not to lend it to anyone."

"Don't lend it," Sam lectured. "Don't lose it. Take real good care of it. It also opens the special cupboard in the equipment room. That's where we lock up all the gloves and other things the players think are special."

"Other things?"

"Special bats, helmets, cleats, whatever."

"How come the players don't keep those things in their lockers?"

"Because they're not really lockers, are they?" Sam explained. "They're just change cubicles."

"I don't understand. Why do we need to lock up gloves? Nobody is going to use somebody else's glove."

"It's a precaution," Sam said. "Two years ago, a fan stole John Hanna's glove. The thief must have jumped the fence during batting practice, and we forgot to lock the dressing room door. Knew what he wanted. Hanna's glove was the only thing missing. Well, that meant John had to break in a new glove. It threw him off until June. His average dropped below .250 for a week."

"I remember that," I said. "That's the only year in his career he hit under three hundred."

"Right. And all because of a new glove. Some players have been using the same glove since they were in college. So, we humor their superstitions."

"Superstitions?"

"Ballplayers are the most superstitious people on the planet, Rob. You take Bubba Jones, our catcher. He comes to the ball park one hour before official practice starts, never early, never late. Then he lays out his uniform on his bench and gets dressed, except for his socks and shoes. Five minutes before he goes on the field, he finishes dressing. Left sock, right sock, right shoe, left shoe. Always the same order. And before he bats, he always touches the water cooler in the dugout. Don't ask him why. He just does it. It's a superstition."

"I always tap the plate three times before I bat," I told Sam. "I have no idea why. But I'm not comfortable if I don't."

"Josh Martin hasn't changed his batting helmet in four years. It's so dirty you can hardly see the Blue Jays decal any more. But Martin thinks if he uses a new one, he'll lose his touch at the plate."

I reached into my pocket and gripped the key in my hand. "I'll guard the key with everything I've got. I don't want anything to happen to the Jays. The team is one of the most important things in my life."

"I know," Sam said. "I could tell by your poem."

"Hey, hey, hey, I want to be part of the Blue Jays," I said. "Huh?"

"My poem."

"Whatever you say, Rob. Now let me show you where to put the bats before a game. Then we'll tour the weight room and see how we shut down after the players leave."

For the rest of the morning and early afternoon, Sam detailed my duties. The more familiar I became with the locker room and Grant Field and having the Blue Jays walking around, the more I enjoyed it.

The practice ended around four and I spent the next half-hour picking up baseballs from every corner of the field and reloading the pitching machines. The players showered, changed, went out for supper and planned to return at 6:30 for their game against the Red Sox.

Sam sent me to collect the water bottles from the bullpen and I noticed the Red Sox bus had arrived and a few players were checking out Grant Field. Robert Yarwood, the Red Sox pitching ace, called me over and asked if I could get him a few new baseballs. It was a small thing, and it only took me a minute, but I pinched myself to make sure it was really true, that I really was part of the team.

"Rob! Hey, Rob!" Cheryl called from the first-base fence, after I handed the baseballs to Robert Yarwood.

I waved and jogged over to her. "Hi! Wait until you hear the neat stuff I've been doing."

"Like losing your pants?" she teased.

"Huh? How did you know about that?"

"I was talking to your friend, Clyde."

"My friend, Clyde? My friend? When were you talking to him?"

"He was sitting on a picnic table. When he saw me, he came over to say hello. He said his mom works in the office and he only lives a block from here and he only goes to school for the first period every morning and his teacher is giving him work to do at home so he doesn't fall behind and his favorite color is orange and he likes cheeseburgers without the onions and he once had chicken pox in an embarrassing spot which he had to scratch all the time and he's going to be a teacher when he finishes college."

"He told you all that?"

"It was an intense conversation. I think he likes me."

"Clyde likes you?"

"When I told him I was with you, he told me all about your day and the joke the team played on you. You must have looked really cute with no pants. I wish I'd seen it."

"Clyde likes you?"

"He said it was so funny, he couldn't stop laughing."

"It happened to him too," I told her.

"Clyde didn't say anything about that. He asked me to go to a movie with him tomorrow night."

"He did? Why would he do that?"

"Because I'm gorgeous and fun to be with. What a stupid question."

"But he doesn't even know you."

"He wants to."

"Clyde could be dangerous. He could be a psycho or something."

"A psycho? He's your friend."

"He's not my friend. Are you going to go to a movie with him?"

"Why?"

"I want to know. Are you going to go with him?"

She scratched the side of her nose as she thought. "Is it any of your business?"

"I want to know," I said.

A smile began around the corners of her mouth, dimpled her cheeks and exploded into a full-blown grin. "Are you jealous, Rob?"

"No."

"You're fibbing. You're jealous. Cool."

"I'm not jealous. It's just that I don't trust Clyde."

"Why?"

"He calls me Poet."

She laughed. "That's funny, considering your poem."

"How would you like to be called Poet?"

"I've been called worse."

"I can think of a few things I'd like to call you right now," I snarled.

"Don't get upset, Rob. I think it's sweet."

"I'm not upset! I just wanted to know if—"

"I told Clyde I couldn't go," she said.

For some reason, I blushed. "Oh. Good. That's good."

"Yes, it is," she said. "I feel much better now."

***

Sam told me to take an hour for supper. Cheryl, Grandpa and I bought hot dogs from the concession and sat in the Jays private box. I told them everything about my day. Then I went down to the locker room to get ready for the game. Only a handful of players were taping knees or ankles, slowly getting dressed. One of them was Clarence Rivers.

"You nervous, kid?" Clarence asked me. "You're pacing."

I told him the truth. "This afternoon was just practice. This is a game. What if I make a mistake?"

"Spring training is the time to make mistakes. This is fun, kid. And you're not going to do anything wrong. You just run out and pick up bats and foul balls. No biggy."

"There will be thousands of people watching to make sure I pick up bats the right way."

Clarence chuckled. "There's always somebody watching. You do something right, you're a hero. You mess up, you're the donkey of the week."

"Thanks for cheering me up, Mr. Rivers."

"No more of that Mr. Rivers stuff," he warned. "My name is Clarence. Use it."

"Okay, sir."

"What?"

"Okay, Clarence."

***

Sam Morris showed me how to move the Jays game bats from the equipment room to the dugout and arrange them, by the player's uniform number, on the bat racks. As I placed Josh Martin's bat into the slot, I examined the scuff marks. I wondered how many of those smudges were home runs. I raised the bat to my shoulders.

"Rob Carter is at the plate. The bases are loaded," I said out loud to myself. "It's the bottom of the ninth. Jays are behind 5–2. The count is 0–2. Yarwood, the Red Sox pitcher, is smoking them. His fastballs are over 95 miles an hour. Here's the wind up. The pitch. It's an inside fastball. Carter swings and—"

"It's a home run," another voice finished.

I turned around, completely embarrassed, to see Sam Morris dropping a pile of towels on a bench. "Nice hit," he said.

"I, er," I stuttered. "You must think I'm a dweeb."

"A dweeb?"

"A nerd," I said.

"A nerd? I have no idea what you're talking about, Rob. But I do know you have things to do." Then Sam showed me how to space the helmets on the shelves, how to fill the pitcher's rosin bags, how I was supposed to stand in the far left corner of the dugout during the game and a dozen other things I worried if I would remember.

Ten minutes before game time, I took my place on the bench next to the bat rack, wiped my sweaty palms on my pants and wished the butterflies in my stomach would flutter away. Clyde visited me for a moment. "You nervous, Poet?"

I wanted to stick one of the bats down his throat. How dare he ask Cheryl to a movie. Didn't he know Cheryl was…what? Cheryl was what? Cheryl was with me? What did with me mean? This Cheryl and me thing had got complicated all of a sudden.

"No, I'm not nervous," I fibbed.

"You sure look it," he noted. "In fact, you look like the nervous type, Poet."

"If you call me Poet one more time, I'm going to—"

Tom Washington, the Jays top pitcher, didn't let me finish the threat. "Hey, Ron," he said to me.

"It's Rob," I told him.

"Whatever," Washington grunted. "The umpires need the keys to the batters' box. Josh Martin has them. Find him and get them."

"You bet," I said. I knew Martin was down by the left-field foul pole signing autographs, so I ran full out to the outfield corner. "The umps need the keys to the batters' box," I told him.

Martin smiled, took off his hat and wiped his forehead. "The keys to the batters' box, huh? Let's see. I gave them to Sanchez a half-hour ago."

I glanced back to the dugout. Edgar Sanchez, the Jays shortstop, was doing stretching exercises beside the cooler. I hustled at full speed toward him. Sanchez appeared a little startled to see me. "How come you're running?" he asked.

"I need the keys to the batters' box," I panted.

Sanchez smiled, then he turned and called to Clarence Rivers, "Hey, Clarence, what did you do with the keys to the batters' box?"

I wondered why Clarence wore a sympathetic expression when he answered, "I gave them to Yarwood on the Sox."

"Gee kid," Edgar Sanchez said. "I know it's your first day, but how can we start the game with a locked batters' box? You were supposed to get the keys to the umpires a half-hour ago."

That shocked me. "I was? Sam didn't say anything about that." Great. Now I had something to really worry about. I was screwing up. Why hadn't somebody told me about the keys to the batters' box? I charged toward right field and the Boston bullpen, to all-star pitcher, Robert Yarwood.

Yarwood was starting the game that evening and he was in the middle of his warm-up. "Excuse me, Mr. Yarwood," I interrupted. "Edgar Sanchez told me you have the keys to the batters' box and I need them to give to the umpires right away."

"Not this one," Yarwood muttered to himself. "Every time I come to Dunedin." He shook his head. "I don't have time for this. Think about it, kid."

What did he mean by that? I needed those keys in a hurry. I glanced toward home plate. The managers were meeting with the umpires and exchanging line-ups. I had to hurry.

"Who has the keys to the batters' box?" I shouted to the Red Sox pitching staff.

They started laughing.

I ran to the Boston dugout, almost in a panic. "Who's got the keys to the batters' box?" I yelled.

Again, everyone began laughing.

I ran past the umpires and back to the Jays dugout. "I can't find the keys to the batters' box," I announced. The Blue Jays players couldn't hide the smirks on their faces.

"Why are you running around like that?" Cheryl was standing to the left of the dugout.

"I've got no time," I wheezed. "I need the keys to the batters' box. I need them in a hurry."

"The what?"

"The keys to the batters' box. The umps need them to start the game."

Cheryl stared at me, as if she couldn't believe what I'd just said. "Rob, think for a sec. Where's the batters' box?"

"I have no time, Cheryl."

"Where exactly is the batters' box?" she repeated.

"It's on both sides of home pla—" I thumped the side of my head and looked at the Blue Jays players. Now they were laughing like the Boston team. "How could I fall for something so stupid?"

The batters' box isn't a box. It's the name given to the place next to home plate where the hitters stand.

"They got you again, Poet." Clyde stated the obvious.

I became aware of the thousands of fans, drinking soda and beer. I cringed. Had they been watching me? Fortunately, the crowd had their eyes on the players. I breathed a sigh of relief, which didn't do anything to help my embarrassment. I grimaced at Cheryl and slunk into the dugout.

"I fell for that trick too, Poet," Clyde told me. "'Course, I caught on a lot faster than you did. You're kind of slow, huh?" I shot him an angry scowl.

Josh Martin patted my shoulder sympathetically for the second time that day. "It's part of the fun. Enjoy it."

"How many more tricks are there?" I asked.

He grinned. "You've paid your dues. Now let's whip the Red Sox."

I returned the grin with a pained smile. "It sounds a lot better than running all over the field."

6

A Slimeball

We did whip the Red Sox, 11–5. I quickly discovered that a spring training game isn't a real game. The Jays regulars only played a few innings; the coaches were letting them get into shape slowly. Most of the game was played by guys from the triple and double A leagues who were in camp for a look-see.

But it was still exciting. After I ran out and picked up my first bat, I lost my nervousness and got right into it. If I may allow myself to brag, I did an XL job. The Jays treated me as if I'd been with them for a season, rather than a few hours.

When I walked out to retrieve the rosin bag after the Jays had retired the Sox in the ninth, Cheryl and her grandfather stood up in the private box and gave me a standing ovation. "You were great." Cheryl flashed one of her patented smiles and, immediately, I wore a Dumbo grin.

I was trucking the bats back into the equipment room when Edgar Sanchez said, "You did good, son. We played a couple of tricks on you and you took them like a pro. And you worked a fine game. We're always glad to have someone like you on board."

My grin was so wide my face hurt.

As the players showered and joked around, Sam, Clyde and I stacked the bats. Then we locked up the gloves, special helmets and batting gloves and whatever else the players were

superstitious about in the special cupboard. Actually, cupboard was the wrong word for it. It was a huge, free-standing
metal locker, so thick and heavy you'd need dynamite to blast
it open. "Nobody could get into this without a key," I noted.

"Right," Sam said. "That's why you don't lend your key
to anyone."

After that chore, we tidied the weight room and collected
the empty juice cups from the lockers and benches. By the
time we were done, the players were gone.

Mr. Jim Dennis came to congratulate me for doing so
well. He told me he'd sent Cheryl and her grandfather home,
and that he'd give me a ride to North Redington Beach when
I was finished for the night, since it was on the way to his
condo.

"See you tomorrow, Poet," Clyde called as he slipped out
the door and walked home.

"Don't call me that!" I shouted, but Clyde left before he
heard me.

"You get all the towels from the bullpen, Rob?" Sam
Morris asked.

"I'm pretty sure," I answered. "I'll run out and check."

The lights were still on in Grant Field, although the place
was deserted. The ground crew had laid the tarps, and it was
hard to believe there had been thousands of people watching a
ball game less than an hour before. I checked the benches in the
bullpen. As I'd thought, I'd collected all the towels.

"Hey, son," a voice called.

I looked around to see who it was.

"Over here."

I saw a man standing outside the chain-link fence behind
the third-base seats. "You got a minute?" he asked. "I'd like to
talk to you."

I walked over to check him out. He was short, shorter than
me, pudgy and very bald. His tanned head reflected the play-

ing lights. The guy was dressed in white slacks and shoes with one of those loud checkered sports jackets. He looked like a used-car salesman in a TV sitcom.

"Is there a problem, sir?" I asked.

He flashed a toothy smile. "I was watching you tonight, son. I haven't seen you before. You new around here?"

"My first day."

He acted surprised. "Your first day? I thought you were a new face, but I had no idea it was only your first day. I saw you and I said to myself, 'Herb, there's a young man who knows what he's doing.'" His accent was definitely southern. "Herbert Abernathy is the name. My friends call me Herb. Who do I have the pleasure of speaking to?"

"Rob Carter."

"Where you from, Rob? You're not a local."

"I'm from Canada."

"Canada, you say. That's one of my favorite places."

"Have you visited Canada?"

"Not exactly, but I plan to one day."

"Do you need any help with anything, Mr. Abernathy?"

"Mr. Abernathy? That sounds so formal. Call me Herb."

I pointed to the empty stands. "Everyone else has gone home."

"I know that. But I was hoping you and I could have a private little talk."

Instinctively, I backed away from the fence. Was he one of those weirdo guys?

"You see, Rob," Mr. Abernathy continued, "I am a procurer of collectibles. I represent several wealthy clients who collect baseball memorabilia. Do you know what that is?"

"Sure, old trading cards," I answered reluctantly.

"That's a part of it, son. My clients aren't only interested in baseball cards. They buy bats, hats, uniforms, bases, gloves — anything that has special importance to the game. I wonder if you'd like to help me out and, in the process, make yourself some substantial dollars."

"I think you're talking to the wrong person. I'm just a batboy for the week. The public relations manager is still in the ballpark. I can go get him for you."

He shook his head slowly. "No, no, no, son. You're in a much better position to help me. Let me be more specific. You ever hear of Mickey Mantle?"

"Course."

"Roger Maris?"

"You bet. Maris broke Babe Ruth's record for the most home runs in a single season in 1961. Some people think Josh Martin may pop the record this year."

"That's right, Rob. Some people do. In fact, some people are betting on it. Mickey Mantle and Roger Maris, they were part of the best hitting outfield in history. I bet there hasn't been a better batting outfield until...until the Blue Jays outfield this year. Josh Martin in left. Calvin Hobbs in center. And now that they've signed free agent Marcus Nicholas, they have three guys, all .300 plus hitters, all long ballers. Maybe all three of them can break the home run record."

"Could be," I agreed.

"Do you know if I had Roger Maris's glove from 1961," Abernathy declared, "I could sell it to a client for thousands of dollars? Maybe, tens of thousands? And if I had Mantle's glove, I'd have a bidding war on my hands. Do you understand what I'm saying?"

I shook my head.

Abernathy heaved a frustrated sigh, tucked some of his stomach into his belt and removed a wad of money from his pocket. A major wad, all fifties and hundreds. "What I'm saying, son, is I'm willing to pay substantial dollars for the gloves of three certain outfielders. If these outfielders do as well as some of my clients are betting, then their spring-training gloves, the three gloves as a set, are going to be worth a pretty penny. You getting my drift now?"

"You want me to steal Josh Martin's glove? And Hobbs's and Nicholas's gloves too?"

"No, no, no, son, steal is the wrong word. I'd like you to see those gloves go missing and in return..." He waved the money at me.

I turned and walked away.

"Wait, son," he called. "Don't look so shocked. You've got me all wrong."

I glanced back at Herbert Abernathy as I entered the dugout. He climbed into a white Toyota. The car engine fired to life, and he fishtailed out of the parking lot in a spray of gravel.

I found Sam Morris folding towels from the dryer. "You were gone a long time, Rob."

"Sam," I said, "there was this guy outside who offered me money if I stole baseball gloves."

Sam arched his eyebrows. "He still there?"

"No, he took off."

"What did you say to him?"

"Nothing. I walked away. The guy was creepy."

"Good move, Rob. We run into guys like him every once in a while. Walking away is the best thing to do."

"Can't we do something about him?" I asked. "He wanted me to steal gloves. Can't we call the cops?"

"It would be your word against his," Sam said. "He'd deny it all. There's nothing the police could do. But if you see him again, tell me. I'll make sure security kicks him out of the park."

I pointed at the special cupboard. "Locking up the players' stuff is a smart move," I said. "The guy was a sleaze, Sam."

"I suppose in a way, it's a compliment," Sam Morris reasoned. "If we weren't the hottest team in The Show, the guy wouldn't be here."

***

Jim Dennis drove me back to Cheryl's grandfather's place. "Just forget it," Mr. Dennis said after I told him about Herbert Abernathy. "We probably won't see him again. Other than that, how was your first day?"

"Super. I had two practical jokes played on me. I was batboy for a great game and I got to meet the Blue Jays. It's been the best day of my life."

"We'll make sure tomorrow is less boring then," he joked.

***

When I got back to Cheryl's grandfather's house, Grandpa had already gone to bed. Cheryl was sitting on a deck chair next to the pool, dressed in a bathing suit. "Robster!" she said when she saw me. "You're back. Cool. Go change and we'll go for a swim."

"You're wearing a bikini," I noted.

"I'm glad you noticed. Do you like it?"

"It looks fine."

She snapped her fingers. "Fine. That's it? It looks fine? I was hoping you'd say it looks sexy."

"I, er…"

"Don't stand there acting like you've been run over by a bus. Go get changed. Let's swim."

"Now?"

"No, next week. Come on, Rob. I've been waiting an hour for you. Move it."

***

Ten minutes later, Cheryl and I were treading water in the deep end of her grandfather's heated pool. "This is great, huh?" Cheryl said. "It's only March and it's hot. It's weird swimming outside when it's early spring in Toronto."

"This whole thing is weird," I replied. "If you had told me last Christmas I'd be batboy for the Blue Jays in March, I wouldn't have believed it."

"Hey, Rob," Cheryl said. "Grandpa's asleep. No one can see us here. You want to skinny-dip?"

"What?"

"Let's go skinny-dipping," she said. "Like the fish do."

"Skinny-dipping? Me and you?"

"No, you and Godzilla."

"Are you serious?"

"Kind of."

"You are?"

She dove under the water and surfaced a quarter minute later. "I only said it because I knew you'd have a cow."

"I've never been skinny-dipping," I said. "Have you?"

"Sure."

"You have? When?"

"A long time ago. In third grade. I spent a couple of weeks in Camp Keenooshayo on Lake Joseph in Muskoka. Everyone snuck out of the cabins and swam naked in the lake. It was so dark, I couldn't see anything interesting, if you know what I mean. Are you shocked?"

"Definitely." I swam to the shallow end, boosted myself out of the water, sat on the edge and watched Cheryl swim over. She hitched herself out of the pool and shuffled beside me.

"I like it here," she said. "I even like the palm trees."

"I guess I acted dumb when we first got here, huh? Sorry, I was just excited."

Cheryl brushed wet hair out of her face. "I thought it was kind of interesting to see a palm tree too. It's neat to see them growing along the side of the road."

"Why were you giving me a hard time, then?"

"Because when Robert Carter is acting like a dork, it's my duty to dump on him."

"Thanks a lot."

"You're welcome. Look, Rob, I'm good for you. Back in fourth grade, before we became friends, you were always uptight about everything. I taught you how to relax. Proof is how well you handled the batters' box thing. And losing your pants. You got over that real fast."

"And I owe it to you?"

"Most definitely."

"I suppose I can add modesty to your good points."

She laughed.

"Guess what happened as I was cleaning up tonight," I said.

"You were hit by a meteorite?"

"Pardon?"

"How am I supposed to guess what happened while you were cleaning up? It's a pretty stupid question when you think about it. Why don't you just tell me what happened?"

So I did. I told her about Herb Abernathy and how he wanted me to steal the gloves.

"And you just walked away?" Cheryl asked when I was finished.

"Yeah, the guy was a slimeball."

She splashed the water with her feet. "Maybe, but the guy sounded like a rich slimeball. Was the wad of bills really big?"

"I'd guess over a thousand dollars. But he didn't say how much he was going to give me."

"Then I would have asked him," Cheryl said. "If it's substantial, like you said, it might be worth lifting a few old gloves."

"You think it's okay to steal?"

"They're just old gloves."

I detailed the facts about ballplayers' superstitions and how it took months to work in a new glove and how players got attached to their equipment and how John Hanna was in a slump for most of the season when he had to break in a new glove after his old one was stolen. "...and I can't believe you think it would be okay to steal something."

"Everyone has a price," she pointed out.

"You don't really believe that. You're just saying that to get me going."

"Darn it. You're catching on," she said as she slipped back into the water.

7

Missing

Clyde Pitman was getting dressed in his batboy uniform when I walked into the Jays locker room the next morning. "How's it going, Poet?"

"Listen, Clyde, don't call me Poet. I wrote one poem to win a contest."

Clyde reached into the breast pocket of his T-shirt and pulled out a baseball card in a plastic envelope. "You want that?" Inside the plastic protector was a mint Mickey Mantle, a head shot in a red circle.

"It's a 1959 Topps," Clyde said. "You collect cards? You want that one?"

"Sure, I collect cards. But only new stuff. I don't have anything this old. Thanks."

Clyde waved the card in front of my face. "Nice joke, Poet. I'm not giving it to you. It's for sale. If you want it, it'll only cost you three hundred."

"Three hundred bucks?"

"Market value. Check the price guide."

"That's too rich for me. And you're still calling me Poet. Would you stop, please?"

"I wish I had Mantle's rookie card," Clyde said. "In mint condition, it's worth nearly ten thousand. Can you imagine that? Ten grand for a baseball card?"

"It *is* kind of dumb," I agreed. "I heard Wayne Gretzky paid half a million dollars for Wagner's card."

"It's not dumb," Clyde disagreed. "It's smart. There are only three Wagners in the whole world, and Gretzky has the only one in first-class shape. Ten years from now, it's going to be worth a million. You play it smart, you can make major cash selling sports stuff."

I thought about Herb Abernathy and his offer for the gloves. I figured it was a good thing the guy had spoken to me instead of Clyde.

Clyde slipped the card back into his pocket. "Well, if you change your mind, you know where to find me. Say, Poet, I was talking to this babe for a few minutes yesterday."

"A baby?"

"Not a baby. A babe. You know, a girl. Great looking. Cheryl something. She said she was from Canada and came to Florida with you. That true?"

"Yeah, Cheryl is with me."

"She your woman?"

"My woman? What are you talking about?"

"She your girlfriend?"

"My girlfriend? Not really."

"Either she is or she isn't."

"We're close friends. Real close."

"But you're not going out?"

"Why do you want to know?"

"Because there's a dance at my school on Friday. I want to ask Cheryl. When the guys see me walk into the gym holding her hand, they won't believe I got so lucky."

"I don't think—" I didn't get a chance to finish the sentence because Sam Morris bounded into the locker room. He was amazingly swift for someone with such a massive stomach.

"Morning, gentlemen," Sam greeted us. "Clyde, the laundry truck just arrived. Go help unload. Then sort out the clean uniforms and stack the towels."

"Sure thing, Boss," Clyde replied.

Gerald the caterer entered the clubhouse carrying the food cooler. "Chili and fresh rolls today," he said.

"Clyde," Sam continued. "Fifteen minutes before lunch I want you to start microwaving the chili."

"You got it." Clyde left to help with the laundry.

"Rob," Sam said. "Today is just a workout day. No game scheduled. But be ready to do the batboy thing. I have a feeling Yancy Hutchins is going to call a squad game this afternoon. You're in charge of the special cupboard this morning. Open up and start passing out the gloves."

"Yes sir, Boss," I said.

I walked into the equipment room, reached into my pocket to remove the key and inserted it into the lock.

"Hey, Rob," Josh Martin called from behind me. "You got the keys to the batters' box?"

I turned around and smiled at him. "I gave them to Edgar Sanchez. Why don't you go ask him?"

Martin returned the smile. "You're going to do okay, kid. Hand me my glove, please."

I removed the lock and the heavy metal door squeaked open. I knew something was wrong, even before I figured it out. The locker didn't look the same as when we closed it last night. It was somehow lopsided, unbalanced.

I found the strip of masking tape with Martin's name scratched in ballpoint pen. No glove. The shelf behind it was empty. I glanced down to Calvin Hobbs's name. Again a shelf minus a glove. I checked for Marcus Nicholas's name. I knew before I looked I'd find a naked space. The gloves of the Toronto Blue Jays outfielders were all missing.

8

A Perfect Plan

That evening, Cheryl and I sat on the picnic table beside her grandfather's pool eating the spaghetti dinner she'd cooked. Grandpa had gone out for his bridge night.

"So what did the police say?" Cheryl asked.

"Basically, they said there was nothing they could do. They said they'd keep a look-out for Herb Abernathy's white Toyota, but since they didn't have a licence plate and there are thousands of white Toyotas, they doubted they'd find him. And even if they did, they wouldn't be able to do anything unless they found the gloves."

"It has to be him," Cheryl reasoned. "First, the guy asks you to steal the gloves, and then they're the only things missing."

"The cops didn't seem all that eager to do any detective work. One of them told me the gloves may have been special to the players and collectors, but the fact is, they were just hundred-dollar ball gloves."

"Were you scared when the cops were grilling you? Did they shine a light in your face?"

"Of course not. And they didn't *grill* me. It was more like an interview. They interviewed everyone who had a key to the clubhouse and the special cupboard."

"Who had a key besides you?"

"That's the problem. All sorts of people. Sam Morris, of course. And Clyde. The manager, Yancy Hutchins. All of the coaches. Jim Dennis. Even Clyde's mother had one, although she can't remember how she got it. To make things worse, the cops found a spare key hanging behind the weight room door."

"Doesn't sound like much of a security system."

"The lock was meant to stop someone from outside walking in and stealing the equipment. It wasn't meant to stop someone in the organization."

"An inside job? Why do you think that?"

"When I opened the locker this morning, it was locked. Sam said the locker room was locked. How did anyone from outside get in? And if you were stealing something, you'd want to get away as fast as possible. Why would you bother to lock up after yourself?"

"You're right. It must have been somebody allowed in the locker room. Wow."

"Yeah, wow."

"How did the players take it? How did they react when they found out their gloves were missing?"

"Everyone tried to make like it was nothing, but I could tell Calvin Hobbs was upset. Marcus Nicholas said he had planned to break in a new glove this spring anyway, but I think those were just brave words. And Josh Martin went through practice in a blue funk. I can't see how it won't affect them. Sam says we shouldn't make too much out of it, but I know he's worried. It sounds corny, but we'll have to hope for the best."

"You're right. It does sound corny." Cheryl finished the last of her spaghetti. "You want to get changed into our swim stuff and get wet?"

"We only just ate."

"Your point is?"

"We have to wait an hour before going in the water."

"That's just an old wives' tale, Rob."

"No, it isn't."

"Fine. We'll wait, Mr. Cautious."

"I know who did it, Cheryl. I know who stole the gloves from the locker and sold them to Herb Abernathy."

"You do? Did you tell the cops?"

"No, because I don't have proof."

"Who was it?"

"Clyde."

"Clyde?"

"Clyde Pitman. Who else would want to steal them? Sam? Mr. Morris? The players? They wouldn't hurt the team for a few hundred dollars."

"A few hundred buckaroonies sounds good to me."

"Sure, it does. That's because you're thirteen years old," I pointed out. "A hundred or a thousand dollars is big-time change to people our age. That's why it has to be Clyde."

"Or you. If you want to use that logic, you're a suspect too."

"I'm trying to be serious, Cheryl. It was Clyde."

"Did Abernathy talk to Clyde?"

"Not according to him. Clyde told the police he hadn't seen the guy. I had the feeling he wasn't telling the truth."

"I don't think so, big guy. Clyde is too nice."

"Nice? Why do you think that?"

"Because he called me just before you and Grandpa came home. We talked for a long time."

"He called you here? How did he know the number?"

"I gave it to him yesterday."

"Why did you do that?"

"Because it's a free country."

"I don't like it, Cheryl. You can't trust Clyde."

"You don't like it because Clyde is a boy."

"That's not true."

"I like it when you get jealous, Rob."

"I'm not jealous!"

She smiled.

"Did Clyde ask you to the dance at his school on Friday?"

"How did you know that?"

"He told me he would. He said he was going to walk into the gym holding your hand and show you off to his friends."

"He did? Is that a compliment or an insult?"

"He can't be trusted, Cheryl."

"Maybe. Maybe not. Like you said, you can't prove he's a thief."

"I'm going to prove it," I asserted. "Tomorrow, I'll show everybody it was Clyde who stole those gloves."

"You will? How?"

"You can help me. Listen…"

***

Grandpa dropped me off at Grant Field at noon on Wednesday. Then he and Cheryl went to lunch and planned to return for the game against the Phillies at two o'clock.

As the players arrived, Clyde and I handed out the towels and uniforms. A locksmith had changed the lock on the special cupboard. Sam kept the only key. I set up the bat rack for the game, arranged the helmets and placed the Gatorade bottles in the dugout. A half-hour before game time, Clyde and I finished our chores. "Hey, Clyde," I said, "you want to take a break? Get a soda?"

Clyde looked at his watch. "Sure, we got time."

We took a couple of drinks from the cooler in the locker room and went outside to sit on the picnic tables. I popped the tab on the can. "What do you think about the stolen gloves, Clyde? You got any ideas about who took them from the locker?"

"Who knows? You want to hear something funny, Poet? At first, I thought you were the thief."

"Me?"

"Then I thought there's no way a guy who writes poetry would steal anything."

I pinched my chin as if I had a heavy thought. "To tell the truth, when Abernathy flashed that money at me, I was tempted. I mean, they're only old ball gloves."

Clyde's face was etched with amazement. He placed his soda can on the table. "You're kidding."

"No, it's the truth," I lied. "Since the gloves have vanished anyway, I'm sort of upset it wasn't me who got the thousand bucks."

"A thousand!" Clyde gasped. "That jerk only offered me four hundred." He suddenly looked confused. "Oh, geez, guess I said something stupid, huh?"

I played coy. "Didn't you tell the cops you hadn't met Abernathy?"

Clyde nodded. "I did. But I was scared, Poet. I love this job. I didn't want to lose it. I mean, who looks the most suspicious? You and me, right? And if I admitted I'd talked to Abernathy, everybody would think it was me. The cops would say, 'We got two kids. One writes poetry, the other doesn't. Who is probably guilty?' Me, of course. Then I'm fried."

I continued to play my plan. "That's a smart move," I said.

"You think that? Does that mean you're not going to tell?"

"Of course not. You got the wrong idea about me, Clyde. Listen, Herb Abernathy phoned me this morning. He said he wanted Tom Washington's glove and asked if I could get it. Abernathy said the glove of the guy who won the best pitcher of the year award was like gold."

Clyde's eyes were tablespoon-wide. "He did? Did he say he had the outfielders' gloves?"

"I asked him and he laughed. I figure that was a *yes* answer."

"Holy…"

"He offered me five hundred big ones." I pushed the ruse. "And I'm majorly tempted."

"Five hundred bucks," Clyde said. "You're really thinking about it?"

"Why not? Abernathy said he'd be waiting for me in the parking lot after the game this afternoon. It's such easy money."

"How you going to get into the locker, Poet? Sam has the only key now."

"No problem, Clyde. I saw Sam put a spare key in the top drawer of his desk."

"Awesome. You got it all planned."

"I do. If I go through with it. I'm still thinking."

"Five hundred? How can you *not* do it?"

"Hey, guys," Sam called from the doorway. "We got a game in twenty minutes. What are you doing sitting on your butts?"

As we pitched the empty cans in the recycling bin, I said, "You keep quiet about Tom Washington's glove and I promise I won't say anything about you talking to Abernathy."

"You got it," Clyde agreed. "Boy, I sure had the wrong idea about you. Guys who write poems are tough dudes."

***

I did another okay job as batboy, but the Phillies had the Jays' number and trashed us, six to zip. Although the star outfield only played three innings, it was obvious the stolen gloves had upset them.

The Phillies' first hit was a smash to left. Josh Martin jumped up against the wall to snag it and, incredibly, the ball bounced out of his new glove. I thought it could have just been bad luck, but when Calvin Hobbs bobbled a routine fly, I got worried. In the third, Marcus Nicholas collided with Hank Franca, the first baseman, on a blooper. At the plate, Martin, Hobbs and Nicholas were hitless. Things were definitely not normal.

There were a few boos from the fans. I glanced at Cheryl every ten minutes. She was so impressed by the Jays play that she had her face buried in a horror novel.

The manager, Yancy Hutchins, gave the players a royal lecture after the game. He spent a lot of time on "negative thoughts." And how everyone was a pro and how superstitions about gloves were just that — superstitions. And the name of the game was pitching, fielding and batting better than the other team. The mood in the locker room was a meltdown downer.

By seven, all the players and coaches had left. A half-hour later, Sam, Clyde and I were ready to leave. It was time to paint the finishing touches on my plan.

Right at that moment, I was positive Clyde was guilty. He'd fibbed about meeting Abernathy and offered the weak excuse about losing his job. He'd told me about the four hundred dollars he'd obviously received for delivering the gloves. He promised not to tell anybody about my plan to steal Tom Washington's glove. How could anyone be more guilty?

Now I had to do two things. First, I had to make it look like I'd changed my mind, chickened out. That would make it easy for Clyde to take my place and steal the glove. Second, I needed a witness. I'd arranged that with Cheryl. I had told her grandfather I'd show Cheryl the locker room after the players left. Grandpa had left because he knew Mr. Dennis would give Cheryl and me a ride home. Cheryl and I could hide out until we caught Clyde in the middle of the crime. A perfect plan.

9

Locks

O kay, boys," Sam Morris announced to Clyde and me in the dressing room. "That's it. Let's shut her down for the night."

"Okay, Boss," Clyde said. Then he studied me. He glanced at Sam's desk, at the drawer where he thought there was a new key for the large, metal locker. "What are you going to do now, Poet?" Clyde asked.

"I'm going to go back to North Redington Beach where I'm staying with Cheryl's grandfather."

"You don't have any other plans?" Clyde probed.

I shook my head. "No, I changed my mind. I just can't go through with it, if you know what I mean."

He nodded. "Yeah, I understand."

"What are you going to do, Clyde?"

"Go home. See what's on TV."

"I'll see you tomorrow, Clyde."

"Right, Poet. See you tomorrow."

"Be here at ten o'clock sharp," Sam said as we left the clubhouse.

I walked toward Mr. Dennis's office as if I was going for my ride, but I stopped short and hid behind a palm tree. I watched Clyde walk down the street toward his house and waited until Sam's car pulled out of the parking lot. Then I went to get Cheryl.

She was sitting outside Mr. Dennis's office reading a novel. "Hi, Rob," she said. "This is a great book. It's about these two kids in Alberta who meet this grizzly bear."

Mr. Dennis heard us and looked up from the stack of papers that covered his desk. "I need another fifteen minutes to finish up," he called to me through the open door. "Then we'll go home."

"No problem, Mr. D," I called back. "I want to take Cheryl on a tour of the locker room anyway. Now that there's nobody there."

"Sounds good to me," Mr. Dennis said. "Take your time. My fifteen minutes may be more like a half-hour."

***

"I'm hungry," Cheryl said after I unlocked the clubhouse door. "Is there any food in there?"

"No," I whispered. "There's a caterer guy, Gerald, who brings lunch every day. He comes back in the afternoon to pick up the cooler and any food left over."

"Is there any juice then?" she wanted to know. "Something to take the edge off my appetite?"

I swung open the door and gently pushed her inside. "There's juice, but there's no time. Clyde could be back any second."

"I still don't believe it's Clyde. This is a complete waste of time. And why are you whispering, Rob?"

"Because we have to be quiet."

"Why? There's nobody here."

"Because." I closed the door, locked it again, and we entered the locker room.

"Turn on the lights," Cheryl whispered into my ear.

"No, if Clyde opens the door and finds the lights on, he'll

know something is up. Give me your hand and I'll lead the way."

She quickly slipped her hand into mine. "Oh, I like this. Where are we going?"

"Into the equipment room where the special cupboard is. We can hide under the table and wait for Clyde."

"Hiding under a table in a dark room. This is sort of romantic. Don't you think so?"

"Give me a break, Cheryl."

"I guess not," she grumbled. "Rob Carter only thinks about sports. You know, it would be more romantic if the place didn't smell so sweaty. You need to get a can of air freshener."

"Sssh." I twisted the handle of the equipment room door, and it swung open with a dull squeak. The locker room was dark; the equipment room was a wall of solid blackness. I groped my way inside.

Cheryl squeezed my fingers. "Where are we? This is a little spooky, big guy."

"Sssh."

Suddenly, something hard and heavy pounded my chest and drove the breath out of me. Cheryl's hand was ripped from my grasp and I reeled backward. My rear end thumped into Sam Morris's desk. Before I had time to inhale, a hand reached out and searched for my face. Long fingers located my head and the arm attached to the hand twisted around my neck and clamped me in a headlock.

"Rob! Where are you? What's going on?" Cheryl called from somewhere in the blackness. Her voice was muffled by the arm surrounding my ears and skull.

Tiny, silver stars danced inside my squeezed brain. It felt like my head was being cranked in a vise. I punched uselessly into the air, trying to hit my attacker. A couple of times I connected with something hard, which I guessed was a knee-cap. The arm squeezed my skull tighter.

"Give up!" a voice yelled. "I've caught you, Poet. Give up!"

"I found the light switch!" Cheryl shouted.

Instantly, the darkness was replaced by the cool glow of fluorescent lights. The stars in my vision danced over a pair of sneakers.

"Clyde?" I heard Cheryl ask.

"Clyde?" I said myself.

"I'm going to let you go, Poet," Clyde shouted. "Don't try anything stupid or I'll—"

"Clyde, let Rob go," Cheryl ordered. "Let him go right now."

The headlock slowly released and I wobbled upright, rubbing my head and chest at the same time. My breath returned in short huffs. As the stars vanished, I focused on Clyde Pitman's angry face.

"So you decided to do it anyway, huh?" Clyde snarled. "You decided to steal Tom Washington's glove. You scumbag. It's a good job I snuck back in here and caught you." Then he pointed at Cheryl. "How could you trick poor, old Cheryl into helping you do it?"

I tried to speak but I couldn't find enough breath to put a sentence together.

"There's no such thing as *poor, old* Cheryl," Cheryl told Clyde. "I'm here as a witness. Rob isn't stealing anybody's glove. He's here to stop you from stealing the thing."

Clyde scratched behind his ear. "What? To stop me? You think I'd...you think I stole the other gloves?"

"I don't," Cheryl explained. "Rob does. He made up the story about wanting to steal the glove to trick you."

"To trick me? This really stinks," Clyde declared.

I finally managed a deep breath. "Why did you punch my chest so hard?"

"I didn't punch you," Clyde answered. "I head-butted you. I charged in the direction of your voice."

"It sure hurt," I told him.

"Well, it sure hurts how you lied to me, Poet. I thought we were friends. Why would you think it was me?"

"Because you always call him Poet," Cheryl volunteered.

"He wrote a good poem," Clyde explained. "It was meant as a compliment."

"Told you you were wrong, Rob."

I apologized to Clyde. "I'm sorry. I wanted to help the team. I thought everything pointed to you as the thief."

"I'm really hurt," he repeated.

"Accept Rob's apology, Clyde," Cheryl said. "Shake hands or something. You got to hit and tackle him. That's enough punishment for him being a jerk."

Clyde held out his hand and I shook it.

"That's good. Hey, if neither of you is the thief," Cheryl reasoned. "It means there's someone else who—" She stopped in mid-sentence when we heard someone unlocking the main door.

"Someone's coming in," Clyde said. He reached over and flicked off the light.

"Under the table," he whispered. "Get under the table."

We followed his instructions and bashed each other as we fumbled across the room. "Oof." "Ow." Incredibly, we found the table in the blackout and squeezed underneath as quietly as possible. Cheryl bumped her head and swore in surprise.

"Quiet," Clyde and I said together.

The main door opened and through the open equipment room door we saw a flashlight beam search the locker room. Whoever was coming in didn't want to be seen. We squeezed against each other under the table. The beam of the flashlight continued to search the darkness. My first thought was that a security guard was checking out the clubhouse. How were we going to explain the three of us sitting under a table in the darkness?

"You're breathing too loud, Poet," Clyde exhaled ever so softly.

Footsteps clumped through the locker room. The flashlight searched the doorway of the equipment room. The beam ran across the floor and rested on the special cupboard.

"You sure there's nobody around, Gerry?" a voice asked.

"Positive," another voice answered. "Everybody has gone home for the night. The batboys and the fat guy are always the last to leave and they cut out of here twenty minutes ago."

Gerry, I wondered. Gerry? The voice was familiar. Where had I heard it before? I hadn't met anybody called Gerry. In the reflected glare of the bulb's ray, I saw the silhouettes of two pairs of legs.

"That it over there?" the first voice asked.

"Yeah," the second voice answered. "I'm going to turn on the lights." I knew the voice. From where? Instinctively, I pressed myself further under the table. Clyde and Cheryl did the same. The lights flicked on. I noticed Clyde watching the two pairs of jean-covered legs. Cheryl was looking at me, wearing an expression that asked, "What are we going to do now?"

The legs moved past the table toward the special locker. "Just as I thought, Cal," the Gerry voice said. "The new lock is the same as the old one. Just a single tumbler. I can pick this in a minute or two."

"This is a piece of good luck, huh?" the Gerry voice went on. "Who'd have thought guys would pay money for used baseball gloves."

"You got a good thing here," the Cal voice agreed.

"I couldn't believe how easy it was yesterday," Gerry said. "I walked in here with the cooler and the place was empty. Then I used my clubhouse key to open the cupboard. Twist, turn, open, and as easy as that, the gloves are mine. I wrapped them in a towel and walked out. Nobody even looked at me."

Gerry! Gerald the caterer. The guy who brings lunch every day.

"When I handed the gloves to that Herb guy," Gerry said, "he says, 'You go get me some more stuff and we'll talk more substantial dollars.'"

"I love that word *substantial*," Cal said with a wheezy laugh. "Thanks for letting me in on this, Gerry."

"No sweat. I was a little worried they'd put in a better lock, but they cheaped out. I've almost got it open."

At that moment, Cheryl's empty stomach let loose a long, loud rumble. Clyde and I snapped our heads to look at her. She shrugged, shook her head and looked at her gut.

"You hear that, Gerry?"

"Yeah," Gerry answered. "Must be the pipes or something."

Her stomach grumbled again, even louder and longer, almost a belch-like roar.

"There it goes again. It doesn't sound like pipes to me." The Cal legs turned around and began to walk cautiously toward our hiding place. They stopped, the knees bent slightly and a bearded face appeared below the table top. His eyes, half-closed with suspicion, opened wide and white when he saw us. "Holy!" he gasped. "Gerry, there's three kids under here."

10

Hit Him on the Head

Three kids?" Gerry said in amazement. "Where?" He darted over to join his buddy, and suddenly two stunned faces stared dumbly at us.

"Hi, there," Cheryl chirped. "Did you bring us our pizza?"

"Huh?" Cal grunted.

"Hey, I know these guys," Gerry announced, waving a lock pick in our faces. "These are the two dorky batboys."

"Dorky?" Cheryl said. "I think you're making a mistake. I've only known Clyde for a few days, but he doesn't strike me as *dorky*. And as for Rob, well, I can assure you that he may be a nerd, but he's definitely not a dork."

Gerry looked at her like she was talking in alien. "Who are you? What the heck are you talking about?"

"What are we going to do about them, Gerry?" Cal asked. "They've seen us. They must have heard us. What are we going to do?"

Cal looked at Clyde for a few seconds, then at Cheryl, then his eyes rested on me. "We're going to tell these kids if they say anything to anyone, they are going to end up a bad smell in the attic."

"Is that a threat?" Cheryl asked. "You're not allowed to do that, you know. Making a threat is against the law. If your mother could hear you now, she'd be very disappointed."

"What?" Gerry grunted. "You got a screw loose?"

"I'm not going to take that, Poet," Clyde said to me. "I'm not going to let anybody try to scare me. I'm going to do what I did to you a few minutes ago, okay? You think of something to do to the other clown." With that, he exploded from under the table, head-butted Cal in the chest and drove him across the room.

As Cal skidded backward, he waved his arms and legs like a Raggedy Andy. He bounced off the wall, staggered and spun around in a frantic attempt to keep his balance. Before he could recover, Clyde jumped on his back and wrapped his arms around his eyes and face.

Gerry jerked his head to watch his buddy, and immediately Cheryl flicked out her right leg, catching the back of his head with the sole of her running shoe. The caterer sprawled in a heap on the floor, and Cheryl and I scrambled out.

Unfortunately, or fortunately, depending upon how you look at it, Cheryl's boot to the head hadn't done any damage, because Gerry was on his feet seconds later. As we stood up, the guy was in my face with his fists balled like a boxer. "You twerps!" he shouted. "You're going to be sorry."

"We're in trouble now." I pushed Cheryl behind me.

"What are you doing, Rob?" she protested. "You don't have to protect me. Let me at this creep."

I thought that if I charged Gerry like Clyde had done to me and Cal, then maybe I could knock him over. But before I could act, Cheryl nudged in front of me. She grabbed the bucket of scuffed baseballs from the top of the table. "Let's dance, Gerry Baby." She tipped the bucket and heaved the contents onto the floor. Fifty official American League baseballs bounced and rolled around Gerry's feet.

"Just because you're a girl doesn't mean you're going to get away easy." Gerry moved toward her. His foot stepped directly on one of the balls and, just like a character in an old Charlie Chaplin movie, Gerry did an exaggerated backflip.

He landed on the floor of the equipment room with an uncomfortable thud and made a noise like a frog being squashed by a fifty-seat school bus.

"Quick, hit him on the head with a baseball bat, Rob!" Cheryl yelled.

"Hit him on the head with a bat? I can't do that. He could get hurt."

"Look out!" Clyde yelled from his piggyback ride on the blinded Cal. Cal staggered under Clyde's weight, then stumbled and bumbled onto the loose baseballs. Clyde jumped off Cal's back as Gerry's buddy torpedoed headfirst into the special cupboard. There was an unpleasant noise of skull meeting steel, followed by a sad moan. Cal crumpled to the floor.

"Oooh," Cheryl said. "That must have hurt."

Amazed, we watched Gerry lurch to his feet. He eyed his moaning friend, then us, and then his instinct for self-preservation took over. He kicked the baseballs out of his path and barged past Cheryl and me out of the equipment room.

"Get him!" Clyde shouted. "Stop him, Poet!"

Stop him? How?

Instinct made me bend over, snatch a baseball off the floor and chase after Gerry. He dashed through the main door and between the picnic tables. He'd reached the gate in the fence when I wrapped my fingers around the laces and wound back in my best fastball delivery. I flicked my wrist perfectly and the ball smoked through the air. The pitch bounced off Gerry's head and ricocheted into the air like a pop fly. Gerry stopped, rubbed the spot where the ball had hit, then simply sat down on the grass. "This isn't any fun any more," he said.

"What's all the noise?" Jim Dennis came out of his office. "What's going on?"

"We caught the thief, Mr. D." I pointed at the seated Gerry, gingerly rubbing his hair. "He stole the outfield's gloves."

Mr. Dennis went over, grabbed Gerry by the arm and helped him stand up. "Gerald, it looks like we have a lot to talk about." He guided the caterer to a picnic table. "We'll just wait here while Rob calls the police."

"My head hurts," Gerry whined.

"I'll call the cops in a sec," I said and ran back into the clubhouse. Maybe Cal had recovered. Maybe Clyde and Cheryl needed help.

They didn't. Cal sat on the floor, his back against the special cupboard, his wrists and ankles securely wrapped in athletic tape. Cheryl and Clyde stood over their catch like a pair of safari hunters.

"Did you stop the other guy?" Clyde asked. "I was just about to come help you."

"Yeah, stopped him good. Mr. Dennis has him."

Cheryl boogie-danced like a halfback after scoring a TD. "We caught some bad guys. Cool. I always thought I'd make a great superhero."

***

"I'm very disappointed in you three," Mr. Dennis lectured. "No, make that *extremely* disappointed. I can't believe you put yourself in danger like that."

"You were foolish," Mrs. Pitman said. "You had no idea what those men could have done."

Cheryl, Clyde and I sat in Mr. Dennis's office getting royal heck. The police had picked up Gerry and Cal five minutes before and, as soon as they left, the angry words started flying.

"Rob, I'm responsible for you in Florida," Mr. Dennis went on. "When I think about what could have happened I have to shudder."

"I understand that," Cheryl spoke for the three of us. "We wouldn't have been in the locker room if we knew Gerry and Cal were going to show up. It's like we told you. Rob was there to catch Clyde. Clyde was there to catch Rob. The real thieves were a surprise."

"Still, you attacked *them*," Mrs. Pitman pointed out.

"It was self-defence," Clyde told his mom. "We were trapped after they heard Cheryl's stomach."

"I'm still hungry," Cheryl interjected.

"Everything worked out okay," I said. "Except for the bump on Gerry's head, nobody got hurt."

"I'm pleased you discovered the thieves," Mr. Dennis said. "But I want you to promise you'll never do anything like this again."

Clyde, Cheryl and I nodded in unison.

"What's going to happen to the bad dudes?" Cheryl asked.

"The police aren't sure," Mr. Dennis said. "They didn't steal anything tonight, so they can't be charged with theft. They didn't really break and enter either. They were just trespassing."

"What about picking the lock?" I asked.

"That counts as vandalism," Mr. Dennis answered. "You said you heard Gerry say he gave the gloves to Herb Abernathy, and Gerry doesn't deny it. But the cash value of those gloves is under five hundred dollars and that's just a misdemeanor in this state."

"What does that mean?" I wanted to know.

"Not all that serious," Mr. Dennis explained. "It means if Gerald offered to pay for new gloves, they'd probably let him go."

"That doesn't seem fair," Clyde said.

"Maybe the cops will catch Abernathy," Cheryl said. "He can't be too far away if he's expecting Gerry to get him more stuff."

"I have a strong feeling Mr. Abernathy will be a long way away the moment he hears Gerry is talking to the police," Mr. Dennis observed.

"I sure hope I didn't hurt Gerry bad," I said. "I really nailed him with that baseball."

"He was more stunned than hurt," Mr. Dennis assured me.

"I think it's time we all went home," Mrs. Pitman said. "It's been quite the day."

"Okay, everyone," Mr. Dennis said. "Remember tomorrow is a day off. Right now I think we deserve it."

Clyde and his mother left and Mr. Dennis locked up the office. As we walked through the parking lot, Cheryl slipped her hand into mine. "This week is turning out to be even better than you thought, huh?"

11

No Goofy?

On Thursday morning, my day off, Cheryl and I were delighted when her grandfather surprised us with a trip to Disney World. After breakfast, we piled into Grandpa's car for the two-hour drive to Orlando.

"This is great, Grandpa. Just super," Cheryl said as we pulled into the parking lot of the Epcot Center theme park.

"It sure is," I added from the backseat. "I really appreciate this, Grandpa."

Cheryl twisted around to look at me. "You *appreciate* it? What kind of comment is that? That sounds so boring. Get a little excited, Rob."

"I am excited. That's why I appreciate it."

She turned around, shaking her head. Then she glanced out the window. "Holy! Look at the size of this parking lot. There must be a thousand cars here."

"Probably three or four times that many," her grandfather guessed.

We parked, walked to the road that divided the huge lot in two and caught a shuttle bus to drive us to the gates. Then we waited while Grandpa bought the tickets. As we walked through the gates, a smiling Disney employee handed us pamphlets on Disney World.

"Who was Epcot anyway?" I asked Grandpa.

"He wasn't anybody," Cheryl's grandfather answered. "It's all in the booklet. Epcot stands for Experimental Prototype Community of Tomorrow."

"Wow, check out the big silver dome," Cheryl gushed. "I've seen that on TV lots of times."

"Pretty impressive, huh?" Cheryl's grandfather noted. "There's two parts to Epcot. Right now we're in Future World. Believe it or not, these big buildings are rides. You line up at the door, hop on the seats and you're entertained for the next ten minutes. The other part of the park is called World Showcase. Several countries have buildings to promote themselves. Canada has a pavilion."

"Sounds like it'll take us all day to see everything," I said.

"I don't want to disappoint you," Cheryl's grandfather warned. "But you can't do it justice in one day. I'd suggest you do the rides here, then maybe catch the movies in the Canadian and Chinese buildings." He looked at his watch. "By then, it'll probably be dark. I'll meet you back by the front gates at seven, okay?"

"Aren't you going to stay with us?" Cheryl asked.

Grandpa smiled. "You young folks don't want an old-timer following you around. I'll see you later. Enjoy yourselves." With that comment, he turned and vanished into the crowd.

"Where do you want to go first?" I asked Cheryl.

"To the bathroom," she answered. "I see one over there. I'll be back in a minute."

I sat on a bench and read the pamphlet. Then I relived last night's adventure in the Blue Jays dressing room in my head. I pictured Clyde on Cal's back, Gerry slipping on the baseballs, me whacking the caterer with my best pitch. Nobody back in Toronto was going to believe it.

When Cheryl came back, I noticed her expression was a little less beaming. "Is something wrong?" I asked.

She searched the crowd. "Well, it's weird that I haven't seen Mickey yet."

"Mickey?"

"Mickey Mouse. And Donald Duck. And where's that magic castle thing you see on TV?"

I held up the pamphlet. "The castle is in another part of Disney World called The Magic Kingdom. I read about it."

"You mean I'm not going to see Goofy?"

"I think The Magic Kingdom is for the little kids," I guessed. "Epcot sounds like it's more for adults."

"I came to Disney World and I'm not going to see Goofy?"

"I don't think Goofy fits in with the Experimental Prototype Community of Tomorrow."

"No Goofy?"

"Goofy is just a guy dressed up in a suit, Cheryl. It's no big deal."

She held her hand at waist level. "Ever since I was a little kid this big, I've had a thing for Goofy. He was my hero."

"You know, that doesn't surprise me, Cheryl."

She grinned. "I guess that's why I like you so much, Rob. You remind me of my hero."

"Huh?"

***

There were huge lines at every building, but we moved quickly. We managed to ride Communicore, Spaceship Earth, The Body Ride, Universe of Energy and the World of Motion before Cheryl's hunger forced us to search for a cheeseburger.

"This whole place is kind of like being in a video game," I said as we ate lunch on one of the outside tables. "Did you see the hologram phone in the future living room? Wasn't it awesome?"

Cheryl nodded. "Not as awesome as meeting Goofy would have been."

I squeezed a ketchup package onto my fries and watched the hundreds and hundreds of people strolling by. Whenever I see a big crowd, like when I go to the Sky Dome, I'm always amazed by how people come in so many sizes, shapes and colors. If you ever tried to describe an average human being to an alien, you'd have a difficult chore. And I've always been fascinated by how certain things in a big crowd will catch my eye. How I'll notice somebody's hairstyle, or smile, or the way they walk. And at that very moment I noticed something I'd seen before.

I saw a tanned, bald head in the middle of the crowd of tourists.

I stood up quickly. "It's him."

Cheryl turned and surveyed the people. "Who? Did you see Goofy?"

"No. It was Herb Abernathy, the guy who paid Gerry and Cal to steal the gloves."

Cheryl squinted her eyes. "Come on, Rob, that's a bit of a stretch. I mean, why would he be here?"

"He has to be somewhere," I reasoned. "I saw his bald head."

"You saw *a* bald head. Look around. Bald heads are like palm trees around here."

"It was him," I insisted. "It was Abernathy." I squeezed through the bushes that surrounded the restaurant patio and ran into the crowd after Abernathy.

"Rob?" I heard Cheryl call from the table. "Where are you going, Rob?"

It took me half a minute to realize I'd lost Abernathy. The tanned, shiny head could have turned in any direction and there were so many people. I searched in vain for another few minutes before returning to the restaurant. By the time I got back, Cheryl had finished her fries and was halfway through mine.

"I was hungry," she apologized. "I'll buy you some more."

I sat down. "It's all right."

"So it wasn't Abernathy?" Cheryl asked.

"I lost him."

"Rob, think about it. You must have made a mistake. Abernathy being in the Epcot Center today is too much of a coincidence."

I knew if I thought about it, I'd have to conclude Cheryl was right. But I wasn't running on reason at that moment, I was flying on *feeling*. I felt that the head I'd seen in the crowd had Abernathy's face under it. I wasn't going to let Cheryl convince me.

"He's the person who has the gloves, Cheryl. I bet those gloves are in his white Toyota out in the parking lot. We've got to wait by the exit for him to go out."

"No way," she said. "I'm not going to wait by a dumb exit for a bald-headed guy who is probably not Abernathy. Maybe I didn't get the chance to see Goofy, but I'm having a great time. Who knows when I'll get to Disney World again?"

I stood up again. "Hold on. We don't have to wait for him. Let's go find the Toyota ourselves."

Cheryl gagged on a French fry. "Pardon? You want to go search for a white car in one of the world's biggest parking lots? You heard my grandfather. There's thousands and thousands of cars."

"Let's go."

"Whoa!" She held up her hands. "Even if the bald head was Herb Abernathy, and that's a big *if*, what are you going to do if, and that's a big *if*, you manage to find the car?"

"I'm going to get the gloves back."

"You're going to break into the car?"

I nodded.

"You're going to break into somebody's car? You?"

I nodded again. "Let's go."

Cheryl grabbed a handful of fries and followed me through the bushes out of the restaurant. "Didn't we promise we wouldn't do something like this again, Rob?"

"Trust me," I said.

***

We had our hands stamped at the gate so we'd be able to return to Epcot, and I marched into the parking lot with Cheryl mumbling beside me. "It must be the sun," she said. "Rob has sun stroke. You don't act like this."

"Let's start on this side of the center road," I directed. "You walk down this row; I'll walk down the next. We'll do every other row until we find the white Toyota."

She peered across the rows of cars that seemed to stretch forever. "One little problem, big guy. What does a Toyota look like?"

I pointed at a blue car, a few spaces away. "It was like that one. Only it's white. See: it's got the name *Toyota* on the back."

"Look for *Toyota*. I think I can handle that."

We began to walk down the aisles of parked cars. We completed the first row and moved to the second with no luck. On the third row, Cheryl called me. "Rob, I think this is one."

I jogged to where she was standing. "You're right." I noticed a little kid's car seat in the back and a half-empty box of disposable diapers. "This isn't it. I don't think Abernathy uses diapers."

It took us fifteen minutes to find another white Toyota. This one had a pile of comic books and games in the back — travel toys for kids. I ruled out that one too. Five minutes later, I found a third car, but it had Ontario licence plates. Abernathy had a southern accent. And he said he'd never been to Canada.

We'd been searching for over an hour and we'd covered less than half the lot when Cheryl called to me again. When I threaded my way through the cars and reached her, I knew we'd hit payoff. "This is it!" I yelled. "That's his sports jacket on the passenger seat."

She peered into the window. "That's a very tacky jacket."

"I recognize it, Cheryl."

"I owe you an apology, Rob. You were right. You do know your bald heads. What are we going to do now?"

"Get the gloves," I told her as I pulled on the trunk. Of course, it was locked, so I tried all the doors. They were locked too.

"You do know it's against the law to break into some-body's car?"

"I'm not stealing anything. I'm trying to take back what's already been stolen."

"I'm not sure a judge will agree with your logic, Rob. Let's not get into trouble. You stay here and I'll go back and get the cops. Then we won't get thrown in jail."

She was right. "Good idea."

Our luck was about to change.

"What have we here?" I recognized Herb Abernathy's voice and turned to see the chubby thief approach the car. "If it isn't the new batboy from the Blue Jays. I remember you, son. And it looks like you have a young lady with you." He bowed to Cheryl. "Herbert Abernathy is the name. My pleas-ure to meet such a lovely young thing. What's your name, darling?"

Cheryl just stared at him.

"Cat got your tongue, I see." He pulled a handkerchief from his pocket, wiped it across his bald head and returned his attention to me. "All right, son, I would like you to explain what you two youngsters are doing around this fine automobile."

"We're trying to get those gloves back," I told him. "We know you have them. Gerry told the police."

"He did, did he?" Abernathy chuckled. "I guess I can't deny it then, can I?"

"I want them back."

"Do you, now? And how do you think you're going to do that?"

"I...I..." I stuttered.

"Exactly," Herb said. "Now suppose you youngsters get out of my way."

I moved to block his path.

"Rob, don't be stupid," Cheryl said.

"But the gloves—"

"The gloves are not worth getting hurt over," she pointed out.

"A smart young lady. You listen to her, son." Abernathy threatened me with a stare.

Reluctantly, I moved aside.

"That's a good batboy." Abernathy flashed his greasy smile as he opened the door.

"I'm going to rush back and call the police," I said.

Herb laughed. "By the time you do that, I'll be a long way away. And I don't think the cops are going to get all that excited about three old ball gloves."

"We know your licence plate," Cheryl said.

Abernathy laughed again. "Wrong, young lady. You know the licence plate of a rented car. Old Herbert is involved in many activities besides acquiring collectibles. He's careful about the cars he drives and the names he uses when he rents them. I'm afraid the licence plate is a dead end. Now I'm going to have to say goodbye to you good children." He inserted the keys into the lock and opened the driver's door.

There had to be some way to stop him. I wished I had let the air out of a couple of his tires. Then my eyes came to rest on the side of the front seat, on the two tiny levers near the floor. They were like the ones on Dad's car. I remembered what Mom had said when she came into my room to tell me Jim Dennis had called. She'd pulled the wrong lever by mistake and opened the trunk, instead of the gas cap.

As soon as Herb put his right leg in the car, I dived at the door. Before he could pull himself in, I reached the levers beside the driver's seat. I wasn't sure which one was for the gas cap and which was for the trunk, so I yanked them both upward. There was the sound of springs as the gas cap and trunk popped open.

I jumped up and darted to the back of the car. In the trunk I saw a suitcase and a ripped, half-full plastic garbage bag. I saw brown leather through one of the rips. Baseball glove leather. I grabbed the bag. "Run!" I shouted to Cheryl.

I hurtled around the next car and into the next aisle. I glanced over my shoulder and saw Herb in hot pursuit. "Come back here!" he screamed. "You're going to be sorry."

I saw Cheryl running toward Epcot to get help.

Dodging cars and running full out, I clutched the garbage bag to my chest and headed back toward the theme park too. But Abernathy wasn't giving up. He was moving quickly for an out-of-shape, middle-aged slimeball.

An exiting car almost ran me over, and the sharp detour forced me to lose ground. "I'm going to get you!" Abernathy hollered.

How was I going to shake him?

Abernathy screamed a string of impolite words at me.

I twisted left and ran down the aisle toward the center road. I thought if I could get to the shuttle bus, there'd be people to help. Abernathy wouldn't be able to do anything with lots of people around.

And then, just as I'd done in center field a few days before, I tripped. This time, I couldn't blame it on the too-long legs of a too-long uniform. I simply got tied up in my feet and flipped onto the asphalt. My palms and knees scraped painfully across blacktop.

As I struggled to stand, Abernathy's hand grabbed my T-shirt. "You little snot!" he shouted into my ear. He reached to grab the gloves. The garbage bag was violently snatched from my hands. But Abernathy didn't have the gloves; Cheryl did.

"I thought about going to get help, Rob," she said. "But I couldn't leave you alone. Whether you know it or not, you need me."

"Give me that bag!" Abernathy howled at her.

"Come get it," Cheryl taunted.

I hoisted myself to my feet, frantically twisted sideways and left a hunk of my T-shirt in the pudgy guy's hand.

"Run to the shuttle buses!" I shouted at Cheryl. We charged neck-and-neck toward the center lane. Herb ran after us, but the exercise was finally getting to him; we were making distance. "We're going to make it, Cheryl," I coached. "Keep running."

A brown car pulled out in front of us and we had to make a panic stop to avoid flying over. I glanced over my shoulder. "Oh, no," I groaned. Abernathy was closing; he was going to catch us.

The doors of the brown car flew open and two people hopped out. Two people wearing pants with a stripe on them. Florida State Trooper uniforms. "Hold it right there!" one of the uniforms ordered. "We want to speak to you."

12

My Poem

A nd then what happened, Rob?" Josh Martin asked.
"Well, it turns out the State Troopers were there because
someone had seen us checking out the cars. And they'd re-
ported us to the police."

"So the cops were after you?" Edgar Sanchez mused. "I
always thought you looked suspicious, Rob."

The players, coaches and trainers in the clubhouse exploded into laughter.

"As soon as Abernathy saw the cops," I continued, "he
started running away. It took Cheryl about ten seconds to
explain what was going on. The police booted after him. Herb
Abernathy didn't get a chance to leave the parking lot."

"You sure had a more exciting day off than I did,"
Clarence Rivers grinned.

There was a murmur of agreement from the rest of the
Jays. The entire team was sitting in the locker room listening
to my story and had been since they'd arrived that morning.

"I don't know about you, gentlemen," Rivers said, "but I
think Ace here deserves three cheers. Hip, hip…"

The cheering was so loud that the walls seemed to vibrate.
"Ace?" I wondered.

"We heard how you pegged Gerald the other night," Josh
Martin told me. "We figured you deserved a nickname."

"Thanks." I knew I was wearing my stupid smile again.

"What I want to know is, where's the girl?" Steve Walton asked. "It sounds like Cheryl deserves a round of applause too."

"She's in the office with her grandfather and Jim Dennis," I said. "She can't come in the locker room."

"Why not?" someone asked. "We're all decent."

"Except for Clarence Rivers," someone shouted out. "He's never decent."

There was a rumble of laughter. "Hey, you guys," Clarence complained.

"Go and get Cheryl," Sam Morris told Clyde. "Tell her to come into the locker room."

"Right away, Boss," Clyde said.

Three minutes later Cheryl, Grandpa and Jim Dennis joined us.

"Hi, everybody," Cheryl said, and again there were cheers and applause, as the players waved their fists with enthusiasm.

"Cool," Cheryl noted. "Maybe I can be a batgirl after all."

Manager Hutchins broke up the celebration. "Enough clowning around. Now we sweat. Outside, everybody."

There was a quarter minute of good-natured grumbling, then the Toronto Blue Jays Baseball Club rose to their feet and clicked from the locker room on their cleats.

After they'd left, Clyde came over to Cheryl and me. "Way to go, guys," he said. "I'm proud to be your friend." Then he smiled. "Here's a couple of passes to the school dance next Friday. You know, I'm really glad I know you, Rob."

"Rob? You just called me Rob instead of Poet."

Clyde thought for a moment. "Cheryl told me how much it bugged you. Sorry, I was trying to be nice. I really did like your poem."

"Hey, hey, hey, I want to be part of the Blue Jays," I said.

"Huh?"

"It's my poem," I explained.

"I don't remember that part." He frowned.

"Come on, boys," Sam Morris called. "We still have a job to do."

"Give Rob a minute," Jim Dennis said to Sam.

"No problem," Sam nodded as he and Clyde followed the team.

"I'm still not entirely happy with the way you went to search for Herb Abernathy's car," Mr. Dennis said.

"We didn't think we'd run into Abernathy," Cheryl pointed out. "We've told you that."

"And as soon as we found the car, we were going to call the police. Abernathy surprised us," I added.

"Which is not his real name, Rob," Mr. Dennis explained. "The police phoned about fifteen minutes ago. It seems our Mr. Abernathy has an extensive history of fraud and petty larceny. The gloves were just a sideline."

"He's wanted in five different states," Cheryl said proudly. "We caught an important criminal."

"And in recognition for what you did for our team, I have an announcement," Mr. Dennis smiled. "The Toronto Blue Jays have decided to give each of you a pair of season tickets to the Jays home games."

"Outstanding!" I said.

"Thanks, Mr. Dennis, that's great," Cheryl said. Then she looked at me and winked. "Just great."

"The only problem is that Rob won't be able to enjoy his seats for most of the year." Mr. Dennis shook his head as if he was disappointed.

"What do you mean?" I asked.

"Well, you're doing such a good job for us that the players want me to ask if you'd like to help out in the equipment room for the home games this summer."

"You mean for the regular season?"

Jim Dennis smiled and nodded. "Exactly. As soon as you finish school for the summer, we'd like you to help us. Interested?"

"Is there any doubt?" I exclaimed.

"We'll talk about it some more later," Mr. Dennis said. "And now, why don't you take this opportunity to show Cheryl the locker room in the daylight, Rob. I'll treat Mr. Robinson to lunch and a beer."

"I can go for that," Cheryl's grandfather declared.

"You're smiling stupidly again," Cheryl informed me.

"And, oh, by the way." Jim Dennis removed a folded magazine from the inside of his sports jacket. "Here's a copy of the souvenir program. It just arrived this morning." He handed it to me. "It's got your poem and picture in it, Rob."

"And remember, I want you to change into that oversized uniform after the game. We have to get a photo of that," Grandpa said as he and Jim returned to the office.

"Hey, Rob, I'd really love to see the weight room," Cheryl said quickly.

"Just a minute." I started to flip through the pages. "I want to see my poem in print."

"Show me the weight room first," she insisted.

"Patience."

"I have to go to the bathroom," she said. "So, let's look now."

I eyed her suspiciously. "What's up?" Then I looked at the program. "You don't want me to read my poem, do you?"

She laughed way up high and squeaky. "Don't be silly."

"Here it is," I said. "There's my picture. And the blurb about the contest. And..." I started to read:

My Greatest Dream

by Rob Carter

We are the Jays of summer,
We are the dreams of fall.
There is no one to doubt us
That we will win it all.

Our pitchers will not falter
Through every season game.
And come the final Series play
The world shall call our name.

Our batters dwarf Mighty Casey,
Nothing can be done;
No opposition can stop us
As we score run upon run.

We are the Toronto Blue Jays,
The greatest team of all,
And when the spirit is needed
We will proudly heed the call.

Come Brewers, Yankees and Indians,
Orioles, Tigers and the rest,
Though you played bravely,
You could not beat the best.

Cheer us from the bleachers,
Let cries echo through the Dome,
Call out our name loudly,
As we bring the pennant home.

Such are the Toronto Blue Jays,
And it is my greatest dream,
To say I was Special Batboy,
And part of the greatest team.

"What's this?" I muttered. "I didn't write this poem."

"I was afraid of this," Cheryl said.

"This isn't my poem," I exclaimed. "Somebody else wrote…" I stared at her. "You wrote this poem, didn't you?"

"Kind of."

"Kind of!" I shouted. "Why would you do this?"

"Keep your voice down. Don't get all excited."

"Don't get excited? How can I not get excited?"

"When you asked me to type your poem, I just couldn't. It really was an awful poem, Rob. So…well, I had this little inspiration and I sent them this one under your name. I thought it said the same thing as yours."

"I won because of your poem," I moaned.

"We're friends," Cheryl said. "Friends help each other."

"What kind of friend would do this?"

"A good friend."

"I'm here because of your entry." I sat on the bench and buried my face in my hands.

"Now, don't start with the honesty bit," Cheryl warned. "Remember most of the other people who entered probably had help too."

"I still have to tell," I said.

She sat down beside me. "I only did it for you."

I looked at her. "You know, I don't know whether to be angry at you or thank you. I feel pretty awful my poem didn't get me here. But at the same time, I'm really glad to be here, even if I do owe it to your cheating."

"It isn't cheating," Cheryl insisted. "The contest asked the person to submit an entry explaining why they wanted the job.

I knew why you wanted the job, and I expressed it a little better. It's not dishonest."

"I still have to tell," I repeated.

"I know. I'll help you explain to Mr. Dennis."

"Thanks. I hope he doesn't get too upset."

"Somehow I doubt it," she said. "Somehow, I think he'll agree with me. Come on, Ace, let's go confess." She smiled.

And, as usual, I started smiling too.

13

I'm On?

Cheryl was right. Mr. Dennis was surprised, but not angry. "The rules didn't say anything about having help with your entry," he reasoned. "So there's no harm done. If Cheryl took your words and wrote them a little better, Rob, then so be it."

But at lunch, Mr. Dennis gave Cheryl a Blue Jays jacket like mine. On each sleeve was the word Helper. "I think we know what this means," Mr. Dennis said.

That afternoon, there was a squad game. The players were divided into two teams, The Blues and The Whites. I bat-boyed for The Blues in the home dugout. Clyde worked the White squad. The Blues had a 7–5 lead going into the eighth. James Henley, who played last year in Syracuse, had gone the distance for The Blues. But he'd given up two hits and a walk with two out, and our bullpen was warming up.

Sam Morris came over to me. "Hey, Ace. They want you in the bullpen."

"They do? Why?"

"Go find out."

I ran down foul territory to the bullpen. Star reliever Frank O'Keeffe was warming up. Clarence Rivers was catching.

"Do you need me?" I asked.

"Hey, Ace," Rivers said. "We were just talking about you. I was saying to Frankie here that you must be one heck of a pitcher."

I looked at Frank O'Keeffe. What were they up to?

"So," Rivers continued, "I said, 'Let's get Ace out here and have him chuck a few.'"

"You want me to pitch?" I asked.

"That's right," Rivers said, as O'Keeffe handed me his glove and the baseball. "Go for it."

"In the middle of the game?"

"Squad game." Rivers smiled. "No big deal."

"This isn't another trick is it?" I wondered. "This isn't an exploding ball? You haven't put Krazy Glue in the glove?"

O'Keeffe and Rivers laughed.

"It isn't a trick," Rivers said. "Although those are good ideas that we'll keep in mind."

"I won't get in trouble with Mr. Hutchins?" I asked.

"Come on, Ace," Frank O'Keeffe called. "This doesn't sound like the guy who captured a ruthless criminal with a hard fastball."

"Okay," I said. "Who am I to argue with superstars?" I slipped on O'Keeffe's glove and placed the ball in the pocket. Then I turned to face Clarence Rivers. "A couple of warm-ups," I called, as I tossed the ball lightly.

"Take it easy on me," Rivers joked.

"Okay," I said when I felt loose. "Fastball, straight on." I dug my foot into the mound and pitched.

"Not bad," Rivers observed. "Can you put it over the outside corner?"

Again I wound up, and the ball sailed perfectly to the outside.

"Good stuff," O'Keeffe said. "At least seventy miles an hour."

"Closer to seventy-five," Rivers disagreed. "I'm impressed, Ace. Can you do a curve?"

"Sure," I boasted.

And I did. I tossed three perfect pitches that broke over the plate. I was strutting my stuff in front of one of the best bullpens in the American League. I couldn't have felt any better.

"What do you think, Frank?" Rivers asked.

"A natural," O'Keeffe asserted. "Let's go for it."

Clarence Rivers turned to The Blues dugout and waved. Immediately Al Johnson, the pitching coach and the manager of The Blues team for the day, walked onto the field toward the pitching mound.

"You're on, Ace." O'Keeffe grinned.

"I'm on?"

Rivers stood up and walked toward me. "Go get 'em, Ace." He patted me on the back.

"I'm on?" I repeated stupidly.

"That's right. We're sending you out in relief."

"I'm on?"

"Come on, Ace." Rivers pushed me toward the playing field. "Consider it our little gift for saving the gloves yesterday."

"I'm on," I muttered as I walked robot style toward the pitcher's mound. The players in The Blues dugout cheered as I approached Henley and Johnson and catcher Bubba Jones.

Henley handed the ball to me. "I'm getting stiff, kid," he said. "Close the inning for me." He left the field.

Coach Al Johnson looked at the scoreboard. "It's 7–5 for us. They've got the bases loaded, but we've got two out. I'm going to put O'Keeffe in next inning. Your job is to get us out of the eighth."

"I'm on," I whispered.

"I know you can do it," Johnson said as he left the field.

"What have you got, Ace?" Bubba Jones asked.

"What do I have?"

"Pitches. What can you throw?"

"A fastball and a curve," I told him. "And a change-up."

Bubba nodded. "We'll stick with the smokers and curves. Okay, let's make it simple. Ignore my first two signs. Two fingers for the fastball, four for the curve. If I touch my mask before you pitch, I want it inside. Touch my chest, it's outside. You got that?"

"I think so."

"Let's get the last out," he coached as he jogged back to the plate.

I threw my warm-up pitches and it suddenly hit me what I was doing. I was involved in a real baseball game with the Toronto Blue Jays. I couldn't believe it. I suddenly wished Cheryl and her grandfather were here to see me. I glanced at the empty stands.

They weren't empty. Mr. Robinson and Cheryl were sitting behind home plate. Cheryl, wearing her new blue jacket, waved to me as if it was normal for me to be on the pitching mound. Her grandfather wore a more reasonable puzzled expression.

"Play ball," the home-plate umpire called.

And then I saw Josh Martin walk up to the plate.

All this time, I had been thinking about what a thrill it was to pitch in a Jays game. I hadn't given any thought to who I was going to face.

Martin tapped his shoes to dislodge the packed sand from his cleats and then took his stance in the box. He made a few practice swings over the plate.

I swallowed. How was I supposed to get a pitch past him? Most of the pitchers in the League couldn't get a pitch past him. Martin looked so powerful, as if he was just waiting for me to give him a pitch he could rip over the fence.

Jones flashed me four fingers on the third sign. That meant curveball. Then he touched his mask. Did that mean inside or out? Whatever, it didn't matter, anyway. Martin wasn't going to miss it. I'd just try to get it over the plate.

The infield shouted encouragement to me. I placed my fingers loosely across the laces, checked the runners, wound up and let go.

The pitch wasn't a bad one, a little up and in, but still a strike. Martin took a wicked swing at it — and missed it completely.

"Atta boy, Ace!" someone called from the infield.

Missed it completely? How could Josh Martin miss my pitch?

Jones called for another curve. This time the ball got away from me and sailed high. Martin let it go.

"Strike him out!" Cheryl called from the seats.

Jones changed the sign to a fastball. I heaved a smoker that bounced on the plate. Two balls and one strike.

"Pick it up," Jones called.

Again the call was for a fastball. The ball was dead center in the strike zone. But I didn't have full stuff on it. It was the type of pitch Martin should have hit to Miami. Instead, Josh did a great fake swing and missed it again.

I waved to Bubba Jones and he trotted out to meet me.

"What's he doing?" I asked. "He should have hit that pitch into Tampa Bay. He's missing on purpose."

Jones flicked up his catcher's mask. "He's just playing along with having you in here. He's just stretching it out. He'll be going after the next pitch. No doubt about that. Don't be disappointed when he knocks the leather off it."

I walked back to the mound. Stretching it out? Knock the leather off it?

Jones squatted behind the plate and called for a fastball. I waved it off. That left my curve. Again I waved it off.

I glanced at Cheryl. She flashed me the magic smile. Then I looked back into the Blue bullpen. Clarence Rivers nodded at me. He knew what I was going to do.

Martin had seen my fastball and my curve. And there was no doubt that if I threw him either anywhere near the strike zone, the White squad would score four runs.

I placed my foot on the rubber, checked the runners again and wound up. By the energy of my delivery, Martin must have thought I was going to offer another fastball. But as I released the ball, I held up and took off all the speed.

The pitch drifted lazily toward the plate. Josh was half-way through his swing by the time the pitch reached him. He ended up in a twisted groan as the ball dropped into Jones's glove. A perfect change-up pitch.

There were hoots from both dugouts. Someone knocked off my hat and rubbed my hair.

"You struck him out!" a voice called.

"Hey, Josh. You miss something?" another voice asked.

"Way to go, Ace! Let's sign him up."

And suddenly, Cheryl was on the mound with me. She'd climbed over the dugout. As she threw her arms around my neck and hugged me, I thought she'd be in trouble. But everyone, including Manager Hutchins, was grinning and cheering.

"You were awesome, big guy," Cheryl shouted in my ear. She planted a kiss on my cheek and we walked off the field. The Blue Jays continued to cheer.

"Just awesome," she repeated.

"Thanks. You know, there's something I've been thinking about the last few days. There's something I have to say. I'm sorry, Cheryl."

"Sorry?" she puzzled. "For what?"

"I'm sorry I didn't get you anything for Valentine's Day," I told her. "I should have got something for my girlfriend."

Cheryl grinned. "I've been waiting for you to say something like that."

"I've just been a little baseball crazy."